CW00525612

Chris never shirked from a challenge. Gay, capable and an achiever, she rapidly made a name for herself in the advertising industry in South Africa, becoming managing director of a below-the-line agency at the age of 26 and retiring at 48 to live in the bush. Passionate about wildlife, Chris transports readers (with humour) into the adventures and trials experienced in a private game reserve in Botswana.

ELEPHANTS
IN MY SALAD

SOME WILD TALES OF LIFE IN THE AFRICAN BUSH

CHRIS BURLOCK

AUSTIN MACAULEY PUBLISHERS™
LONDON • CAMBRIDGE • NEW YORK • SHARJAH

A CIP catalogue record for this title is available from the British Library.

ISBN 9781035869121 (Paperback)
ISBN 9781035869138 (ePub e-book)

www.austinmacauley.com

First Published 2024
Austin Macauley Publishers Ltd'
1 Canada Square
Canary Wharf
London
E14 5AA

To Estelle… who has always stood by me… unless we were on foot and elephants were approaching!

My grateful thanks to my fellow Jwala lovers - Elaine, Marcel, Peter, Leolyn and Reana – for enabling this book to be published.

A typical game drive with friends.

Caesar perched on the windscreen as usual.

Our wild, cud-chewing lunch companion, Harry, a massive old eland bull.

When the main rains fell, the flash floods were both awe-inspiring and dangerous.

After the rains, some areas of bushveld can be transformed with the blooms of the Devils Thorn weed.

The author with the first Range Rover

Estelle just before we left Jwala

Elephants drinking from the Jwala pool. He huge dead Leadwood trunk that was thrown into the pool just visible behind the closest ele.

A typical school outing.
Jim on the left and the staff ladies in the back row

Jim freeing a disgruntled blood-soaked vulture from inside a dead elephant's rib cavity.

Crossing the Limpopo River by from South Africa to Botswana via the pont.

Caesar on a game drive

Just rescued from the swimming pool.
Mpho's forehead and front legs still raw and feet pads white from his ordeal.

Cheetahs on their kill.

Unloading the first of over 20 trailer-loads of materials needed to build our house. Estelle varnishing window frames.

Spot...hand reared...our first house guest.

Finished at last!
Looking from the kitchen towards the bedrooms.

Below: Our lapa on the right leading to the living area and bedrooms. My studio on left.

Where it all took place –
Jwala Private Game Reserve, Botswana

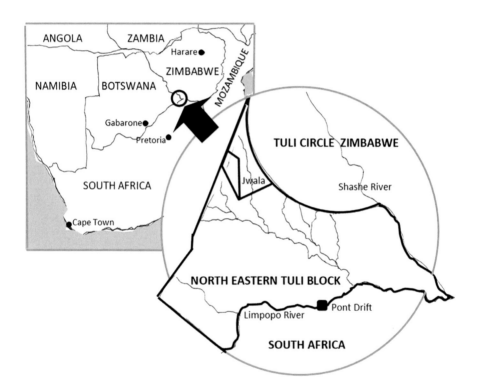

Chapter 1
A 120-kg Abandoned Baby!

It was the terrifying screaming and trumpeting of an elephant that forced me awake. It was still dark and yet warm and cloying, typical of a Botswana summer. In a half-asleep state under the obligatory mosquito net, all I could imagine was that an elephant was being attacked by lions. This would be most unusual in this part of Botswana but why else the blood-chilling noise? If it was indeed lions, walking from my house towards the bellowing was obviously not a safe option, so still battling with my conscience, I stayed in bed. After a while, the noise mysteriously stopped as suddenly as it had begun. Quiet returned to the Botswana bush.

But at seven o'clock when staff members on the private game reserve started their day, they came rushing to my house shouting that there was something in the swimming pool…a baby elephant!

Elephants, even one just a few weeks old, are excellent swimmers. But this was a massive swimming pool a good 20 meters long and some 8 metres wide with very narrow steps into its depths. When I got to the poolside, it was obvious that this little one had been swimming for hours. His forehead was raw from rubbing against the pool sides and the pads of his feet looked like white cottonwool from prolonged water exposure.

The huge pool was an even bigger mess!

In her attempts to rescue her baby, the mother elephant had ripped up great slabs of slate paving and concrete and thrown them into the pool. A large, thatched sunshade had been torn out of the ground and was now sinking in the deep end. But most impressive of all her efforts was the giant Leadwood tree trunk now firmly residing on the pool floor. This massive dead trunk had been lying alongside the pool for probably forty years and was wide enough for one person to lie on to sunbathe and long enough to accommodate two. (In time, it took a massive tractor and eight men to remove it!) Nonetheless, and completely out of character for strongly bonded matriarchal herds, the baby's mother and herd had obviously given up trying to rescue him and had taken off into thousands of hectares of bush, leaving him paddling for his life.

Seeing the little one was in the shallow end, I jumped into the pool and shouted to the staff to help. With me shoving from behind and a strong Botswanan at each ear, we muscled some 120 kilograms of pachyderm onto dry land. The staff all backed off, but the little fellow was determined to join up with its new 'herd', thus my partner Estelle and I became his new moms. Mpho ("Gift" as the Setswana staff had now named him) proceeded to follow Estelle and I everywhere…bleating with hunger. He definitely did not want to be abandoned again!

What do you feed a baby elephant who was obviously still totally reliant on its mother's milk and who had no idea on how to use its trunk to drink water or to feed on grass or leaves? This was way before the days of cell phones and internet. I got onto the radio system that linked several game reserves in the Northern Tuli Block.

Feedback included not cow's milk…only goat's milk…or try brown rice gruel. One piece of advice from the manager of a large reserve was a heartless: "just abandon him. He won't survive… they never do!" (I later learnt that this seemingly cruel suggestion came from an individual who had tried to rear a similarly young motherless elephant that even slept on his bed. But after some weeks, it had died, leaving his foster dad heartbroken.)

In haste, we made up what we could from our pantry: brown rice gruel. As the lodge generator only ran from 6pm to 10pm daily, gruel-making required boiling the rice on a gas stove then pulling up our little petrol generator for the power needed to operate a high-speed blender to turn the soft-cooked rice into the consistency of milk.

This gooey mess was poured into a 2-litre plastic cooldrink bottle. Fitting a calf-teat to the bottle neck, we popped the rubber teat into Mpho's open mouth.

To begin with, Mpho was very pleased with this regime…but after a litre, he concluded it was not what he really needed and chomping down on the teat, he pulled it off the bottle. About 10 times a day, Estelle or I would land up with a sticky mess running down our bare legs and into our sandals! Gruel in between one's toes is not a pleasant sensation.

But his need to feed was evident. When in the lodge lapa (a large sitting/dining area with no walls but a thatched roof nestled on a framework of dark gum-poles), Mpho would sidle up to a vertical gum-pole and then reach up as if the pole was his mother's foreleg …surely there should be a teat there somewhere? It was just heart-breaking to watch. Even big, dark knobs on a chest of drawers were given a suckle.

Fortunately, we did have electrolytes in our comprehensive first aid kit, so we bottle-fed Mpho electrolytes and water in between the brown rice slop.

Being a sweltering hot, Botswana summer, all the animals were in desperate need of water. As well as the usual impala, zebra, warthog and wildebeest, several herds of elephants were constantly around the lodge. While one herd cooled themselves off at the waterhole in the riverbed, another would be at a natural mud wallow quite near to the swimming pool, while a third group would be lounging around the swimming pool, pouring trunkful after trunkful of water into their open mouths. This rotation continued day and night.

Hoping that one of the herds might be Mpho's, Estelle and I, along with our very tolerant, Staffie-cross dog, Caesar, spent day one sitting in the shade of a huge tree near the pool in the hope that Mpho would rush to one of the visiting herds for a blissful reunion with his mom.

No such luck. Each time Mpho enthusiastically approached a herd they presumably smelled human scent on his skin and would turn on him, trumpeting furiously. Some even slapped him with their trunks. Each attempt resulted in the herd taking off with great noise and speed. And Mpho running back to his adopted moms for consolation.

A second radio call to other reserves resulted in the advice to boil Mopane tree leaves in water and wash the baby with the infusion to hopefully obliterate any human scent. As Mpho wanted to be in contact with us all the time, we needed to prevent him from reintroducing any taint of humans, so we dressed in hats, long-sleeved shirts buttoned up to our necks, trousers tucked into socks, closed shoes, and rubber gloves—all in 40-degree heat! We looked like a couple of scarecrows.

Mpho went berserk! But it wasn't our appearance that upset him. Since his rescue, Mpho had insisted on being so close to us that he could rub against us and touch our skin. It was this protective clothing that was upsetting him and only once shorts and T-shirts were reinstated did he calm down, sliding his little trunk over our arms and legs for comfort. As he had ignored any visiting elephants while he attempted to get up close and personal with us, we did not try the scarecrow route again.

Trunk to skin contact may well have reassured Mpho, but it felt like being rubbed with a scrubbing brush to us! A baby elephant's trunk is covered with stiff, prickly bristles, so having his trunk up your shorts, inside your T-shirt and around your face was somewhat of an uncomfortable intrusion. And I leave you to imagine just how invasive he could be when we needed to use the toilet or take a bath! Why not close the door, you ask? At some 120 kilograms, Mpho could do some serious damage to a door!

Being just a few weeks old, like any baby, Mpho needed sleep. He would stand still, his eyes slowly closing, and he'd begin to sway. But just as his head dropped, he jerked himself awake. Soon we learnt to just push him gently while he was swaying, and he would roll onto his side and sleep…but for only 15 minutes at a time. And being so young, when he woke, he had to be helped onto his feet. Normally, mom's trunk would help him up, but now it became a two-woman job.

That first night, we decided to move from our house to the lodge to be near to the pool in the hope that Mpho's herd might return. There were no visiting shareholders, so we dragged our dog's bed and a plastic-covered mattress to what was humorously called the 'honeymoon suite', a large, thatched rondavel on the lawn overlooking the swimming pool. No sooner did Caesar curl up in his bed, Mpho would try and join him. Caesar would patiently move across to the large mattress. And Mpho would follow him onto the mattress. This merry-go-round carried on until sleep would overtake the baby, but then only for 15 minutes. And as we had to help Mpho to his feet when he woke, Estelle and I got very little sleep ourselves!

At one point during the night, we heard elephants at the pool. On opening the door, Mpho trotted out with high expectations, only to be rebuffed again. But as he had ventured close to the herd, Estelle and I decided to hide inside our closed Land Cruiser which was parked behind the cottage in the belief that Mpho would not be able to find us and then might try to join the herd again. Crouched down so we were not visible in the vehicle, we suddenly felt the huge 4 x 4 being buffeted and rocked quite violently. Despite not being able to use his trunk to feed, it obviously functioned brilliantly as a scent tracker! He had followed our scent path and discovered our hiding place. We had to exit the Cruiser quite sheepishly before it got dented.

By now, Mpho had developed a worrying case of diarrhoea. Baby elephants need mother's milk, full stop. The most amazing observation, however, was that his excrement did not smell…at all! This genetic ability helps babies avoid attracting prey animals like lions, leopards and hyenas.

Day two. I neglected to say we were also trying to hand-rear a baby squirrel at the same time, requiring many trips between lodge and house where the naked squirrel, looking a bit like a miniature cocktail sausage, had fallen out of its nest in the eaves of our thatched lapa. We had hoisted it back into the eaves in a tiny basket in the hope that his mom would fetch it. But, yet again, it seemed that a mom was having nothing to do with her foolish child. Hourly feeding of a baby squirrel with a tiny syringe and a baby elephant with a 2-litre bottle was taking its toll on us.

Mpho would walk behind me just like circus elephants of days gone by. His front feet would literally scrape my heels he needed to be so close. I thought it might help to walk Mpho into the bush in case his herd might have ventured back to find him. With a game-viewing vehicle escorting us, Mpho and I walked across the dry Jwala riverbed and away from the lodge. Not an elephant to be seen. After a while we turned back. But now there were three bull elephants some 60 meters away at the waterhole. As the Cruiser made its way down into the riverbed, they looked our way. I was sure their eyes open wider as they saw the strangest sight—a slow-moving vehicle with a human walking a few paces behind it and a baby elephant right behind the human. Fortunately, the puzzled bulls left this weird procession alone.

At about midnight on the second night, I heard the familiar tummy-rumble communication often made by a herd of elephants. They were approaching the pool. In the pitch black (remember the generator only ran from 6pm till 10pm), I tiptoed down the lawn towards the pool with Mpho on my heels, literally!

Great, ghost-like shapes were standing in the bushes some 15 meters from the pool. The shapes were swaying silently, deciding whether to risk approaching the pool as there was an obviously mad, half-naked human with a tiny elephant on the other side of the water.

We all stared at each other for a while. Then I decided I needed to get Mpho closer to the herd before it disappeared into the bush. Barefoot, I walked onto the stone paving surrounding pool, Mpho right behind me. But as I crept around the corner of the deep end, I suddenly heard SPLASH! Mpho had fallen into the pool! The herd was now quite restless but intrigued and held their ground.

Okay…how does a 75-kg female get a 120-kg elephant out of a pool? After some experimentation, here's the trick: 1. Lift left front foot onto the pool surround. 2. Lift right front foot onto the surround. 3. Grab the strong sections where the elephant's ears attach to his forehead…and pull!

The herd was fascinated. Estelle, at a safe distance away with a torch, was also looking on. Perhaps it was the torchlight on my face, or perhaps my heavy breathing from the trial and error of getting Mpho out of the pool, but I had managed to swallow a moth. Coughing and spluttering, I tiptoed along the deep end side of the pool, getting ever closer to where the herd were now milling about in consternation. And then behind me, I heard another SPLASH! Mpho had fallen in the pool—again! Coughing, and by now too exhausted to care about the impatient herd close by, I began the newly discovered extraction process… left foot out, right foot out, and a mighty pull at the top of the ears.

Once Mpho was on terra firma, I shouted to Estelle to light my way with her torch. My plan was to run between the pool and the herd, knowing I could leap into the pool if the herd decided to charge. But the plan failed. As I started my dash—SPLASH! This time I grabbed Mpho's flaying trunk and towed him to the shallow-end steps. But as soon as his feet touched the steps, Mpho immediately put on brakes and pushed away. At that point, I had huge sympathy for Mpho's mom and felt like abandoning him myself. But didn't. Thankfully, the elephant herd decided to retreat and disappeared, leaving Mpho, Estelle and I to retire to the honeymoon cottage, wet but intact.

Day three dawned. Unfortunately, the baby squirrel had not survived the night. As Jwala did not have a manager at the time, it fell on me to fetch a diesel mechanic from the Pont Drift border post to service the game reserve's generator; our only source of electricity to cool the Minus 40 refrigerators and to pump our sole source of water from the lodge borehole.

Estelle was left to feed Mpho and keep him amused, although sadly he was growing less perky as the hours passed.

At about 3.30pm, I drove the 27 kms back to the border with the mechanic, a trip that takes around an hour on ungraded rocky dirt roads, through dry riverbeds and often through more elephants, some of which did not like to be disturbed.

When I got back to the lodge at dusk, Estelle was standing on the airstrip with Caesar… but no baby elephant. And Estelle was in tears. I concluded that poor little Mpho must have died.

Sobbing, Estelle explained that she had taken Mpho down to the Jwala riverbed to splash in the pools of water trapped in the rocks. Suddenly, a herd of elephants approached at pace up the river-course. Estelle's only escape was to climb the rickety gum-pole ladder up to a small platform perched in a tall Appelblaar tree nearby. Despite an extreme fear of heights, she had clambered up to the platform. Estelle lay flat on the planks trying to be less visible but she could still see what was transpiring below. Now Mpho, finding himself abandoned, started to scream! Confused, the herd milled around in total panic, adding to the screams and trumpeting.

Estelle could only helplessly look on while some of the young males ripped large tuffs of tall grass out of the ground and began to thrash Mpho with the grass roots or use their trunks to strike him. The matriarch then took off at pace with her herd following. Despite being badly rebuffed, Mpho had determinedly followed the herd as fast as his little legs could manage. As Estelle made her way down the ladder, she could hear the elephants' continued trumpeting and screaming fading into the distance. In tears, and certain that Mpho was lost and in danger of being killed by hyena, Estelle made her way up to the airstrip to await my return.

Calling on our staff and the managerial couple from a neighbouring reserve to help, we took two game-drive vehicles and powerful spotlights and searched long into the night. The elephants and Mpho had vanished. Not a trace.

At dawn, Estelle and I took up the search again but this time looking for circling vultures that would betray where a carcass might be. No vultures.

But here is the amazing part of Mpho's tale: later that day on a neighbouring reserve, a herd of elephants arrived at their lodge-side waterhole. A baby elephant, noticeably weak and very wobbly, was seen approaching every female and raising his head in the hope of suckling. Eventually, and most unusually, one of the females allowed him to feed! He was frequently seen thereafter. One of the few success stories where an abandoned baby elephant survived and flourished!

Chapter 2
Back to the Beginning

So, how did this whole debacle begin? How did two middle-aged women land up as one-tenth shareholders of a 5 100 hectare (12 600 acre) private game reserve in Botswana?

My career was in commercial art and marketing in South Africa. After working at several advertising agencies and being part of the founding team of Game Discount World in Durban, in 1971 I had joined Paton Tupper Associates (Natal), the country's first 'below-the-line' agency. ('Below-the-line' means sales and marketing promotions, packaging design and the like, whereas 'above the line' is a company's mass media advertising expenditure.) At 26, I was dispatched to Johannesburg to open Paton Tupper Associates (Tvl) (Pty) Ltd.

Despite being very young, British, a woman and gay (not a great combination in what was then a very Afrikaans, male-dominated, conservative country), Paton Tupper Associates (Tvl) succeeded and grew to be the biggest below-the-line agency in South Africa. For some 22 years, I arrived at work before 7 in the morning and left well after 10 at night. (My friends said I was wasting the best years of my life… but when I retired at 48 to live in the bush, most of those same friends still had many years of work-life ahead of them.)

While living in Durban, I had been asked by an acquaintance to pretend I was dating a girl that she fancied in order that she could spend more time with this new flame while still being involved with her long-time girlfriend. Being single at the time, I agreed. The four of us spent some enjoyable weekends together. But as the sham continued, I realised that I really liked the 18-year-old Estelle… and she liked me. So, when I was offered the opportunity to open the Paton Tupper Transvaal office in Johannesburg, we left together. We have now been partners for 50 years (with a 10-year break which I can only blame on my crazy working hours.) During our break, Estelle became an air hostess with South African Airways and when we reunited, she was a first-class cabin attendant on overseas flights.

With my company offices in Santon, Johannesburg, it was convenient for us to live near the well-known Kyalami Racetrack in Midrand (so called as it was halfway between Johannesburg and Pretoria). It was also just 20 minutes from Jan Smuts Airport.

The 5-acre smallholding came with a small Spanish-plastered house, stables, ponds galore and ducks. Very quickly I learnt to hate male ducks as they exhibited gender-based violence of the worst kind; literally raping females—even their own ducklings—while on the water and often drowning them in the process. The ducks were quickly rehomed and replaced with beautiful white geese. Geese mate for life!

One dawn in 1989, on driving out of my smallholding to go to work, I saw a dozen white shapes laid out on the ground. Leaping out of my car, I was devastated to see my twelve beautiful geese laid out, stone-dead. Not a drop of blood. Just dead. From the spoor (paw-prints), I could see that a pack of dogs had come up the valley and killed them. For fun.

That night, depressed by the carnage and alone at the office, I picked up a copy of the Farmer's Weekly magazine, famous for their 'yellow pages' advertising section at the back. Looking under "G" for GEESE, my eye was caught by a tiny advertisement headed "GAME RESERVE, BOTSWANA". The price wanted for a one-tenth share of Jwala, a 5100-hectare reserve, was exactly what I had just received as a profit bonus for that year.

Hating the phone, I nonetheless dialled the given number. A male voice answered: "Do you hunt?" he asked.

"NO!" I spluttered in indignant disgust.

"You have just passed the first test," the man replied. Phew!

Shaun went on to explain that there had been thirty-two responses and just two applicants would be shortlisted and flown in his private twin-engine plane to the Jwala game reserve where he and some of the other shareholders would make the final decision as to whom would join their ranks. If selected, that person would not be required to pay for the flight. The looser would need to pay for their share of the flight costs.

After some further questions, the telephonic 'interview' was over. I did not expect a return call; after all, surely the nine existing (male) shareholders would not want a newbie of that dreadfully useless gender who would keep getting lost in the bush, who would not know what to do if an elephant charged, nor be able to change a punctured tyre in the wild or cook a meal over a wood braai…

But to my surprise, some days later I received a call.

"Be at Lanseria Airport at 6.00am Saturday—and pack light!" Shaun said.

I got to the little local airport at 5.00am dressed in khakis and carrying my camera bag with a toothbrush and a change of bra and underpants tucked between the lenses. At 6.00am I was approached by a friendly, well-built man who declared he was Shaun and that I was to wait for a couple of his pals and the other candidate while he fuelled the plane. Eventually, I noticed a bearded man dressed in a white trousers and white and blue striped shirt entering the tiny terminus at pace. Really? Not your typical bush gear! He was also carrying a suitcase. Not exactly packing light! And he was late.

'White pants' raced around the terminal asking everyone if they had seen Shaun. I pretended to closely study a poster on the wall, hoping he would not think to ask me... but he did. Although really tempted to say I believed Shaun had taken off already, I stopped myself. Explaining to my 'rival' that the plane was being fuelled up, we stood together awkwardly until Shaun's jovial friends joined us.

Being 'bush mad', I had been to several South African game reserves, but never to Botswana. I had also flown in small planes before, but always felt horribly ill.

Thankfully, the take-off was smooth and the flight to the Tuli landing strip went well. I feared that 'barfing' into a plastic bag would be a black mark against my bid to become the newest Jwala shareholder. I might have already got one black mark from declining a beer enroute as I am, and always have been, teetotal. My 'rival' joined the others with a beer. A tick for him?

We flew over the Limpopo River and there was the Tuli Block landing strip serving commercial lodges and Customs post. The twin-engine plane had to buzz the landing strip to clear it of wildebeest and zebra. Exciting. (Prey animals often congregate on open spaces so that lions or cheetahs can't sneak up on them, hidden by long grass.) Disembarking, we made our way to a neat hut to await the arrival of the Botswanan Customs and Immigration officials. They arrived with lovely gleaming white smiles and once our passports were duly stamped, we made our way back to the plane basking in the baking sun.

Problem. Shaun could not get one of the engines to start. After a few more attempts, the miscreant engine burst into life, and we were on our way to the Jwala landing strip some 15 kilometres north. When the engine refused to splutter into life, my 'rival' was in a bit of a panic, obviously nervous that this adventure had suddenly become somewhat life-threatening. Black mark against his chances? My philosophy in life is to not worry about things that one has no control over. If an aircraft malfunctions mid-flight, so be it. Nothing I can do.

Seeing Jwala from the air, I became more and more sure that this was my dream come true. Shaped a bit like a wedge pointing north, its curved and unfenced eastern side bordered the Zimbabwean Tuli Circle, its western border was demarcated by a game fence separating the Botswanan Tuli Block game reserves from cattle land. Its southern-most boundary (also unfenced) lay some 17km from the apex. Boundaries of reserves within the Tuli Block are defined by a mere 'cutline' or vehicle track. The cutline between Botswana and Zimbabwe was demarcated by a double track.

Jwala is part of a vast, flat, usually dry grassland, speckled with large patches of Mopani bushes and a few empty streams and riverbeds fringed with larger green trees that have found all-important water deep under the sand and rock-filled, dry water courses. Shaun flew over Jwala pointing out the boundaries. Then the lodge itself appeared below a wingtip. A huge green lawn boasting a massive Mashatu tree dressed in a purple-flowering bougainvillea was partially surrounded by a scattering of large and small thatched buildings. The west edge of the lawn lay a sparkling blue, extremely large swimming pool. On a slight rise above this garden of Eden lay a kilometre-long, dirt runway for light planes which culminated in a huge tin-clad hangar.

After disembarking and unloading cooler bags, my 'rival' and I were taken on a tour of the Jwala lodge. We were shown the large diesel generator which supplied 4 hours of electricity each evening, providing light and more importantly pumping water from a borehole into a couple of huge water tanks standing high on great metal platforms out of reach of elephants. When the tanks filled, the overflow helped supply the waterhole below in the usually dry Jwala riverbed some 70 paces from the lodge. Water was gravity-fed into the lodge bathrooms, communal kitchen and staff 'village'.

The Jwala lodge consisted of a manager's cottage, then occupied by the founding shareholder Roger Petty and his wife Del, who had acquired Jwala for just R49 000 some 10 years previously. The previous owner had wanted to get rid of Jwala quickly as it was rumoured that the manager been hung at the lodge by insurgents during the Zimbabwean War of Liberation. Due to this tragedy, the then owner never stepped foot on the reserve again and sold it to Roger for a song.

To the left of the modest manager's cottage was a hangar-like garage that could house some eight vehicles. To the right was a series of six rustic, thatched double rooms with quite basic ensuite bathrooms. (Tiling was not one of Roger's strengths, bless him!) Hot water was supplied by 'donkey burners'; old metal fuel drums repurposed to hold water with a chimney running vertically through the drum so that water could be heated by a wood fire underneath. Fortunately, Botswana temperatures, even at night, meant that cold showers were popular.

Next was the lapa: a massive, semi-open, communal gathering place with a dining table that could seat twenty at a push. To one side was an impressively long bar counter that Rodger and his son had sawn by hand from a single tree trunk. In the centre of the lapa was a happy mix of donated lounge furniture. Its thatched roof was suspended on dark, creosoted gum-poles in the centre and around the perimeter. The floor was locally sourced slasto; slices of pale ochre-coloured sandstone. At the river-facing end of the lapa was an open-air communal fire pit surrounded by a huge semi-circular stone bench where shareholders and their guests gathered at night to braai (barbeque) and share stories of the day's sightings, or just sit and marvel at the night sky. With the nearest bright lights some 30km away in South Africa, and clouds or rain a rare occurrence, the canopy of stars was always breath-taking and the sight of falling stars a frequent delight!

On the opposite end of the lapa, slasto steps led up to a large 'boma', which consisted of a very large communal lounge, a small dining area, storerooms, and a large, outdated kitchen, all under thatch.

Beyond this communal section was an elongated thatched rondavel (round house) that stood apart and looked down on the pool. Due to its relative isolation from the rest of the lodge buildings, this accommodation unit was jokingly termed the 'honeymoon suite'!

All in all, the lodge was basic, rustic, and utterly charming… and I was even more in love!

Fortunately, my 'rival' seemed less pleased. On our tour of the lodge, he seemed put out by the fact that the massive garage area seemed fully occupied by vehicles… "so where will I park mine?" When the empty plane hangar was indicated (a walk of some 150meters), this did not go down well. A second black mark? He then declared that when he built (each shareholder had the right to build a house near the lodge), he would not be using thatch. He was sharply told by the shareholders present— the judging panel—that thatch was the only option. Ah, a third black mark against him?

Following a light lunch (and more beers of which I did not partake… black mark against me?), Shaun took us on a game-drive in an open 4x4 Land Cruiser. Despite seeing frequent spoor and piles and piles of elephant dung, we did not spot an elephant. Botswana is renowned for its herds of these magnificent animals and has the largest number of free-roaming elephants in the world. But as hunting is allowed in Zimbabwe's Tuli Circle and as the border between Zimbabwe and Botswana's Tuli Block area is unfenced, during the Zimbabwean hunting season, many herds of elephants move to the safety of the Tuli Block but bring with them an understandable aggression towards humans and vehicles. Unlike the herds in South Africa's Kruger National Park, and more especially the fabulous Addo Elephant Park which are so habituated you can almost reach out and touch the animals, extreme caution is required during encounters with pissed-off elies in Botswana!

However, the game-drive did not disappoint with sightings of giraffe, herds of delicate impalas, magnificent spiral-horned kudu. It is said that the world record kudu horns, held in the British Museum archives, evidently came from the Tuli Block. Plenty of zebras and wildebeest regarded us from grasslands and behind branches of butter-fly shaped Mopani leaves.

At one point, Shaun pointed the snub nose of the farm's Land Cruiser down a narrow, twin tyre-track of a 'road' which clung to the west bank of the dry Jwala River. For over 95% of the time, no water is visible in most Botswana riverbeds, but there are obvious signs of water deep under the gravel as large Appelblaar, Mashatu and Fever trees flank their banks. And wonders of wonders, as we bumped and swayed down a small gulley next to the Jwala River, we startled a huge cat that had been sleeping on a limb of a giant Mashatu tree overhanging our path. We saw a flash of pale-yellow belly flying over the vehicle just metres above our heads. With infinite feline grace, the object quickly took off, its black-spotted coat revealing that we had indeed experienced a very close encounter with a leopard!

Even more enamoured than before, I was now desperate to be given the nod to become the tenth Jwala shareholder. The 'judging panel' of three long-standing shareholders took us applicants aside separately to ask us various questions. As the reserve's credo was 'to conserve this wild area for future generations', I felt obliged to confess that, although passionate about conservation, Estelle and I did not have any such 'future generations' in mind as we were gay. (Another possible black mark against me?)

Early the next morning, the hyena-proof wrapping was removed from the plane's wheels and we departed for Johannesburg. Not a hint of whom the judging panel had decided on.

Chapter 3

"You Don't Owe Me Anything"

When we landed at Lanseria, I asked Shaun, "What do I owe you?" Then held my breath.

"You don't owe me anything," was his reply.

Phew and oh wow! I was now a shareholder in a private game reserve in Botswana…all thanks to a cruel pack of dogs that killed my geese!

Estelle was overseas at the time. By now she was a senior SAA air hostess working exclusively on overseas flights. A few days later, I collected her from the airport.

"Guess what," I said as casually as possible, "we now own a share in a private game reserve in Botswana!"

Not sure if she fully comprehended the statement. Nor, at the time, did either of us realise what a life-changer this acquisition would prove to be.

As an overseas flight attendant, Estelle got several days off between her long-haul trips. This, coupled with South Africa's generous public holidays, often gave us the ability to drive up to Jwala for a long weekend. I would pick her up from the airport and she would change into bush clothes while enroute the 5 hour drive to Pont Drift, the most convenient border crossing between South Africa and the Tuli Block in Botswana. The boundary between these two counties is demarcated by the Limpopo River which was mostly dry and therefore one could clear Customs at the SA border post, drive down a concrete ramp, put your vehicle into 4-wheel drive to cross the sandy bed of the great Limpopo River and then up the opposite bank to the Botswanan Customs post.

If the river was in flood, one parked one's vehicle between the SA border post and the river's edge, jumped into the pont (a tiny metal cage suspended on cables) and an old diesel engine on the Botswana side would tug you and your supplies from the large, corrugated shed on the South African side across the Limpopo right into the Botswanan Immigration and Customs post grounds. After the normal border post procedures, a vehicle from your reserve would collect you. Well, that is what usually happened.

Chapter 4
Finding Our Way Around

Once bona fide shareholders of Jwala, Estelle and I couldn't wait to really get to know it.

On our first visit, having not travelled to Jwala by road before, we got lost and landed up at the Mashatu Game Reserve where some surprised staff kindly explained where we had gone wrong. It was with some relief when the Jwala sign carved on an old tree trunk plank came into sight. We were welcomed by a lean and tanned Roger Petty, the original owner and then manager, who offered to drive us around the reserve the next morning.

So early the next morning, we climbed aboard the old Jwala Land Cruiser and Roger drove northwards parallel to the Jwala river-course, pointing out all the trees (which I could never remember) and the various branching-off roads (which I could soon remember). After what seemed to be about 5 kilometres, Roger took a left turn onto a track that led to the tall wire game fence that separates the Tuli Block wildlife reserve area from the rural cattle area which we later discovered was very sparsely populated with delightfully decorated mud huts, small free-roaming herds of cattle the obligatory few goats and chickens.

The contrast in vegetation from the cattle side of the fence and the Tuli Block side was somewhat worrying. Often overgrazed on the cattle side, the Jwala side boasted waist-high, swaying yellow grasses and plentiful Mopani bushes in full leaf. Surely local Botswanans villagers would prefer the fence be removed and the game reserve owners gone. In talking to the locals however, they truly appreciate the game reserves as they provide the only employment opportunities available in the area. Tourism is a vital component of the country.

While driving this boundary path we heard a loud 'fart' from a rear wheel. A huge thorn had punctured the tyre. Roger took one look at the offending very flat tyre and announced that the vehicle did not have a spare nor a jack…we were to walk back to the lodge to collect the same and another vehicle. This walk was our real introduction to Jwala.

Roger pointed out the various spoor and droppings…impala, giraffe, zebra, wildebeest, steenbok… and showed us how one can tell which direction an elephant was walking by the deepest side of its pad-print and the slight impression of its nails. He identified birds new to us and showed us webs of golden orb spiders. He explained why the tall ant hills always curved to point north. (The sun dries out the ants' wet, muddy building extrusions on the sunny side faster than the shade side.) He showed us the burrows of porcupines dug into anthill bases with tell-tale gnawed bones outside…used to keep their rodent teeth trimmed. Other smaller burrows were dug by the rarely seen bat-eared fox; extremely pretty, slight and fluffy insect-eaters who lower their heads until their huge ears hover just over the earth so they can hear any or beetle activity going on under the surface.

Smaller burrows belong to the strictly nocturnal spring hares that hop along on their hind legs just like miniature kangaroos that weigh in at 2,5kg!

Of course, any hole could also be occupied by a highly venomous snake;

a Black mamba, Cape cobra, Mozambique spitting cobra or a variety of adders.

Fascinated with all this information, I no longer worried about Roger's feet wearing only flip-flops across the thorny terrain or the fact that I was hat-less in the strong sun. (I would later pay for the hours of not wearing hats or sun protection with numerous skin cancers.)

On subsequent trips, Roger took us to the very northern tip of the reserve where there was a borehole and large circular concrete water trough. Because this water source was over 15 kilometres from the lodge it was seldom pumped. Introducing water would have resulted in an influx of game and being seldom visited, that would lead to the area becoming a poacher's paradise. As there was no water, there was also very little game. This meant that the grass was tall and thick, and all the bushes covered with leaves. But in the event of a serious drought, a pump would be taken up to this special 'food reserve' and the concrete reservoir filled with water. This ensured that grazers and browsers could move north and eat well, allowing the southern areas to recover once the rainy season arrived.

Once, after some good days of much needed rain, we joined Roger on an inspection drive. Jwala was a mix of a dozen different biomes. In one area there was an annual swamp complete with massive raucous toads who obviously survived the dry summers underground and couldn't wait to go a-wooing in the reed-beds when the rains arrived, and the swamp regenerated. On the opposite side of Jwala was a massive open area with hardly a bush, or any tall grasses; shareholders named it 'the golf course'. And in the middle of Jwala was a fair-sized dam that held water all year round and this was flanked by massive Mashatu trees. Kilometre by kilometre the vegetation differed as the soil changed from sand to rock, from black cotton soil to ochre gravel littered with quartz crystals. Small geodes of low-quality amethyst could also be found in dry streambeds if one looked carefully.

On this inspection drive Roger was in the new manager's Cruiser, complete with cab and doors. Estelle and I stood in the cargo section and held onto the cab roof for all we were worth. This provided us with a great view of the road ahead. I noticed a small terrapin meandering along the muddy track. Roger missed it by a hand's width…then another one…and another. All escaped sure death by inches. When we stopped, I congratulated Roger on his driving skill in squeezing passed all the terrapins. It transpired he did not have his glasses on and had not seen even one!

On another rainy season excursion with Roger, a kudu cow had wandered into deep mud to try and reach water in a pumped waterhole further south. It was trapped and exhausted. Some of the Jwala staff were called in to help the rescue operation. With ropes, much sweat and very muddy legs all round, the kudu was eventually dragged onto firm ground and she galloped off much to the dismay of two hyena nearby who were waiting for the mud to harden enough to allow them safe access to dinner.

We managed to acquire an old game-drive vehicle for our future trips. Although Estelle lived in constant fear of getting lost, we never did. If a dirt track road did not get driven, the grass would take over and the only way to find it would be to walk ahead of the vehicle looking for some signs of where the track might have been. Off-roading was not allowed except in life-or-death situations.

Game drives always produced a new wonder. Like the day when I noticed the head of Black mamba above the tall grass. The snake was keeping pace with us doing, according to the speedo, almost 20 kph. As the grass was some meter high, the snake must have been over 2 meters in length to have its head higher than the grass and still move at such speed!

Then there was the cheetah kill right next to the road. Three cheetahs, probably siblings, had brought down an impala and were recovering from the chase in the shade of a Mopani bush. As Estelle was not with me, I raced back to the lodge to fetch her. To our delight the trio had only just started their meal and ignored our presence. Kills had to be consumed in haste before hyena, jackals, lions, or leopards arrived!

Estelle and I learnt so much about the bush from Roger. He was passionate about the area and infinitely wise… but just not good at managing the expectations of some of the shareholders who could not understand how difficult it might be to maintain vehicles and keep a lodge running with no access to a telephone and the nearest garage half a day's drive away.

Roger had been a schoolteacher and one of the co-founders of Woodmead School back in 1970 when South Africa was deep into its shameful apartheid era. Woodmead was far ahead of its times—educationally, politically and philosophically. It was the first school in South Africa to accept pupils of all races. This move to non-racialism was the fulfilment of one of the major dreams of those who founded the school. It was exciting, but also traumatic with threats from the government to withdraw registration and close the school and even threats of legal action and gaol sentences for the founders.

Woodmead believed that in education it is not the creed, policy or philosophy that matter, but the pupil. "Education for wonder" became its key phrase. The ideal was for every pupil to see life as an exciting challenge which they do their utmost best to meet by realising their own potential to the full. But Roger was soon entrenched in matters that threatened that core foundation. Parents of pupils getting divorced, unhappy and confused children being caught in the middle of the resulting domestic upheaval…and that's when Roger decided to withdraw from his passion and escape from it all. He bought Jwala and put his three children through Matric there. The Petty children all grew up to be charming, bush-wise young adults, and when Estelle and I became involved with Jwala, such were the family ties, all three youngsters were employed and living on different reserves in the Tuli Block.

Chapter 5
Botswana in Brief

Botswana is an amazing country… a place of great stereotypical African beauty with vast deserts, flood plains, grasslands and an abundance of wildlife. I called it 'big sky country' as it is so flat the sky seems to take up more of every vista than is the norm! But as we were to discover, it is the people of Botswana that make it even more special. They must surely be some of the happiest and nicest folk on Earth.

The 2023 census counted less than 3 million inhabitants and an average density of less than 5 persons per square kilometre!

Blessed with a small population and vast natural resources such as diamonds, the government has developed enviable education and medical care systems. In our time there, if a Botswanan needed a treatment for the flu—or a complex brain operation—the fee was the same: two Pula. That was less than R3.00 in SA money or just a few US cents! In times of hardship, small herdsmen were not given handouts of cash but bags of beans! These were to be planted to feed their family and the plants harvested to nourish their cattle.

Predominantly inhabited by people of Tswana origin (collectively called "Batswana"), their recorded history can be traced back to the 14th century. They are believed to be descendants of King Mogale who lived in the present-day Magaliesberg Mountains in South Africa. They migrated northwards, at different times and due to different causes, and established themselves in what was then a relatively unexplored territory.

Towards the turn of the 19th century, the people who resided in the area known as Botswana, made up of several ethnic Chiefdoms whose peoples shared a common language and history, co-existed in relative peace.

During this period, Britain was consolidating its military and economic strength as a major colonial power in southern Africa. At the same time, Dutch settlers calling themselves Afrikaners (Boers) and German settlers in Namibia (then South West Africa) were pushing northwards and westwards, respectively, annexing more and more Batswana lands.

In 1870, three Botswana traditional leaders made representation to the British Government regarding the threat of their territory's annexation by the Dutch and German settlers. With the earnest support of some local British organisations and individuals, the lobby for protection succeeded in 1885, resulting in the Bechuanaland Protectorate.

After 80 years as a British protectorate, Bechuanaland attained self-government in 1965, becoming the independent Republic of Botswana and maintaining a position of stability and harmony ever since.

A map of the Tuli section of Northern Rhodesian (now Zimbabwe) shows a strange anomaly: the border between Zimbabwe and Botswana does not completely follow a river as is often the norm but has a strange semi-circle intrusion across the Shashi River. The story goes that Cecil John Rhodes while laying claim to Rhodesia, put a compass point into Fort Tuli and described a circle around it stating that this circle would be his hunting area! As so it came to pass.

Hunting still persists there and in season elephants move into the neighbouring Tuli Block in Botswana where hunting of elephants is prohibited. These canny beasts entering Botswana bring with them an understandable resentment against mankind!

Yesterday's (and today's) 'Great white hunters' obviously killed those elephants with the largest tusks. Ivory poachers also target the big tuskers. But then something developed in the Tuli region that might save elephants from extinction: a 'tuskless' gene. Often herds are seen led by matriarchs without any tusks. And the calves are often tuskless too. Obviously, these animals are worthless to trophy hunters so will survive to breed.

The only downside, as we discovered, is that tuskless females can be very aggressive. Possibly they are compensating for their lack of 'weaponry'…but being stomped on by a 4-ton elephant is also not a pleasant way to die!

Chapter 6
The Great Limpopo River

When Rudyard Kipling saw the 'great, green-grey, greasy Limpopo River' it was obviously during a very good rainy season. This 1750-kilometre-long river is dry most of the year. When it did flow it could be hugely impressive and often life-threatening.

South Africa had laid a concrete causeway to the centre-point of the riverbed. But Botswana did not take the hint and left their half of the riverbed as sand. When the Limpopo flows, the water is a dense ochre colour due to the sandy soil erosion collected by the heavy rain falls. When the hight of the water is reasonably shallow, 4x4 vehicles can quite easily cross. The downstream edge of the South African concrete causeway is visible as the water cascades over it. But when the water rises higher, that slipway becomes invisible. With no railing or edge-markers, one must just remember or simply guess where the causeway lies. To make matters worse, the roads leading from the two entry/exit points do not line up!

From the South African side, the causeway angles downstream a bit, so one needs to aim a few degrees right and once the concrete ends, one needs to aim a bit left to where the steep road up to the Botswana Customs offices lies.

Once, when the river was running over axel deep, I needed to tow a small truck (called a bakkie in South Africa), up to the Botswana Customs post when the driver had failed to take the dog's leg bend from causeway onto the Botswana side correctly. It was stuck. His passengers, several cheerful mamas bedecked in voluminous colourful dresses, were perched on top of the bakkie canopy to keep dry. Fortunately, my Range Rover had a tow-hitch and the power to rescue the situation. The ladies sang and waved their thanks as the bakkie reached safety. Great fun.

On another occasion, the heavens had opened, and torrents of rain brought flash floods cascading down all the usually dry stream beds. A Swiss shareholder simply had to get back to the South African border as he had arranged for a hire car to collect him and his wife to transport them to Pietersburg (now named Polokwane), and from there, fly to Johannesburg and back to Switzerland. In those days there was no cell signal, and no land line phones, so nothing could be cancelled or rescheduled. A fellow Swiss shareholder who happened to be at Jwala at the same time, heroically decided to try and get Marcel and Ingrid to the South African border post. I joined the expedition in my closed Land Cruiser so that if one vehicle got stuck in mud, the other was there to tow or winch it out. Quickly loading people and luggage we set off in convoy. The Jwala River at least had a concrete causeway, which although already covered with water, was easily crossed. About 9 kilometres further on was the much wider, gravel-bedded Majali River. It was running, but we got through. Reaching the Botswana border post, we could see the Limpopo rising with every passing minute. With passports stamped and warnings not to proceed ringing in our ears, we ventured down the muddy bank and into the froth of the mighty Limpopo River. Fortunately, we found the concrete of the South African causeway and were soon unloading Marcel, Ingrid and luggage at the South African Customs post and beating a hasty retreat back into the swelling river. We wound our windows down in case we needed to exit our vehicles if pushed down river. While crossing, I could see the water breaking over Christopher's bakkie bonnet and up onto his windscreen. Defying all odds his petrol vehicle made it across and so did my faithful diesel Land Cruiser. But I think my hair was distinctly greyer!

When the Limpopo was not crossable by vehicle, the only access was via the 'pont'. This was a small cage suspended beneath wire cables that ran from a large tin shed on the South African side of the river to an off-load point within the Botswana Customs enclosure. A diesel engine on the Botswana side provided the pulling power to transport some 5 or 6 people or goods. During the dry season when the Limpopo was crossable by vehicle, the pont was not in operation which is why the sudden torrential rains we experienced the day Marcel and Ingrid left required the high-risk vehicle crossing.

A year later came the great Mozambiquan floods in 2000. (You might remember the report of a pregnant woman who was forced to deliver her baby while stuck in a tree that she had been forced to scale to escape the flood waters?) Well, upriver from that brave mother, Estelle and I had a less eventful but nonetheless very memorable experience.

Jwala shareholders, Marcel and Ingrid, had very kindly invited us to join them at Lewa Downs, a well-known game reserve in Kenya. We were due to leave Jwala with our dog Caesar, drive down to friends (and voluntary dog-sitters) in Johannesburg, and the next day fly to Kenya. It was the rainy season, and the Limpopo was often running so we had long left our closed Land Cruiser on the South African side.

But the afternoon before we were due to depart it began to rain... torrentially. We decided to leave immediately before the Jwala and Majali rivers became impassable. Using the manager's Land Cruiser which at least had a canopy over the front seats, we wrapped our suitcases in black refuse bags and tossed them into the open cargo area. We got through the Jwala and Majali rivers quite easily and arrived at the Customs post in the dark. Parking right outside the locked gates ensured we would be first through when they opened. Now it was time to try and get some sleep.

Estelle and Caesar slept in the Land Cruiser cab while I squeezed through a gap between the two chained gates and tried to sleep balanced on a narrow wood bench under the eaves of the Customs building. No luck. Whenever the rain let up, I walked to look over the river. The water was getting increasingly high. In my torch light I could see huge trees being swept downstream, roots and branches waving helplessly.

We later learnt that a crocodile farm way up the Limpopo River had been completely flooded, and a slither of happily liberated crocs swept away in the torrent.

Come 8.00am the Customs staff arrived and stamped our passports. I parked the Jwala vehicle up the road, and we got on board the pont which now seemed dangerously close to the great yellow-brown mass of raging water. Hoping to avoid being hit by one of the many dead trees being carried towards Mozambique in the torrent, we thankfully reached the tin shed on the South African side safely.

Our Land Cruiser was parked high on the bank. Unfortunately, some less experienced visitors had parked their vehicles as close to the tin shed as possible—in a dip—and those fancy vehicles were now standing window-deep in muddy water.

When leaving a vehicle parked for sometimes months on the riverbank, one had to disconnect the battery and spray every pipe and wire with nasty smelling Jeyes Fluid to deter mice from gnawing at them. (Jeyes Fluid also stops porcupines from eating plastic water pipes…there's a useful tip!)

Thankfully our Land Cruiser started, and we were soon through SA Customs headed for Johannesburg and a very welcome trip to Kenya. However, when we turned on the air conditioner, there was a strange tick, tick, tick sound which got even faster when the aircon fan was on high. And the more the aircon was on, the worse a somewhat nasty smell emanated from the air ducts. Later, on removing the duct cover, I discovered a very dead, desiccated rat. Its little withered feet had been catching on the aircon fan! Tick, tick, tick!

Kenya was a dream come true. Seeing elephants living side by side with locals, rhino rehabilitation successes and a close-up encounter with their not-so-shy lions at a kill. And a snow-capped Mount Kilimanjaro peeking over the horizon.

After two weeks at Lewa which we will never forget, nor Marcel's generosity in treating us, Estelle, Caesar and I arrived back at Pont Drift only to discover that we had been the last people to leave the Tuli Block via the pont! We were told that the river had risen so high the branches of an uprooted tree had snagged the cables which had to be cut to release the strain. Returning a couple of weeks later, we were also the first to cross back across the river as brand-new cables had just been rigged up.

We heard the funniest story about that flood period. The Botswanan staff at Pont Drift were efficient to a fault. Once the pont was out of commission, a couple of the commercial lodges operating in the Tuli Block realised they were going to have problems collecting their guests from the South African side of the flooded Limpopo River. The obvious answer was to buy inflatable boats (rubber ducks as they are called), to ferry guests and food and drink supplies across the torrent. But once the boats started arriving at the Botswana Customs bank, a studious Customs official did some homework and announced that Pont Drift was not registered as a 'port' and wanted to put an end to this innovative solution! As Pont Drift is several hundreds of kilometres from the Indian Ocean, no wonder it was not a recognised port!

Chapter 7
All Hail Caesar!

I had always loved big dogs, starting with Boerboels (dogs originally bred in South Africa for hunting lions) and then a string of Great Danes. But Estelle had never owned a dog before we got together and subsequently developed such a passion for animals that once we left Jwala and settled back in the Western Cape, she became involved with running and doing hands-on fieldwork for local animal welfare societies.

Fieldwork involves venturing into underprivileged township areas looking for sick, unsterilised, mange-ridden, injured, undernourished or chained-up dogs and puppies. This was both dangerous and heart-breaking work, but she stuck with it for years. When we moved to the Wilderness, she assisted the Garden Route SPCA, becoming a qualified Animal Welfare Assistant. Later she started her own animal welfare in Wilderness, partnering with a delightful township volunteer and continued until the Covid years made that impossible. I tell you this to illustrate that pets are vital to Estelle.

On a visit to Jwala in the early days, we met a couple who managed a nearby reserve and were introduced to their bush-dog: a very cool Staffie-Spaniel mix. Estelle became obsessed with finding such a dog for herself. Back at home, she phoned all the vets in Johannesburg and explored the Classifieds in every local newspaper. Nothing. Then, some weeks later, a vet's receptionist called back. A client's Staffordshire Terrier had been mated by the dog next door; a very determined, wall-climbing Bull Terrier. Of the resulting litter, there was one pup left. The owner might consider selling but was not terribly keen. She gave us the owner's contact number.

A phone call later and we were dashing into the suburb where we were ushered into a tiny backyard. The lawn was smaller than our bedroom at home. And there in the middle stood the ugliest pup I had ever seen! Small and stocky, mostly black in colour with a white flash on its broad chest, brindle front legs and shoulders and some brindle on its cheeks. But Estelle was besotted!

Once the pup's owner heard about the lifestyle it would enjoy on our 5-acre small holding with its ponds, geese, horses, Great Danes and cats, the pup was ours! (Admittedly, we withheld the trips to a game reserve.)

With our new acquisition paid for and safely in our car, we drove straight to our vet to get him checked out and vaccinated. The pup sat on Estelle's lap taking this new experience in his little stride. He passed the wellness exam with flying colours, so the next stop was home to introduce him to his new family. We sat by the swimming pool, the pup on Estelle's lap, when our two Great Danes approached. The tiny black pup had already decided that Estelle was his 'pack' and proceeded to warn off the Danes with some growling and yaps! So, Caesar, our bush-dog to be, joined the family.

To take a dog into Botswana requires documentation from one's vet and then a permit from the state veterinarian in Pretoria. This was a trip that we landed up doing often as the permit expired every 3 months.

Caesar's first trip to Jwala was at some 4 months old. I was repainting the old cabinets in the lodge kitchen when he heard a lion roar nearby. He immediately tucked himself behind my legs, trembling in fear. How did he know instinctively that this noise signalled danger? During our early trips, he seemed totally apathetic towards all other wild animals. I would deliberately drive close to herds of zebra or impala, and he showed no interest whatsoever. Positively yawned.

But then came the elephant chase at night and Caesar suddenly became interested in animals and disdainful of the world's largest land animal! More of that later…

Our game-drive vehicle was an old Toyota Land Cruiser with no cab and no doors. Two raised rows of comfy benches were bolted on the cargo bay section for game-viewing. There was a hand's width gap between the back rest and the bench seating. As a pup, Caesar would go to sleep on the seat, but the constant bump and sway of the dirt track roads would slowly wedge the sleeping pup deeper and deeper into the gap until he fell into the cargo bed and woke with a start.

As he grew older and keener on game-viewing, his new favourite position was sitting or standing on a rubber doormat that we put onto the horizontal glass of the windscreen. (Old model Land Cruiser trucks' front windscreens could be hinged down to lie flat on top of the bonnet.) This platform provided prime viewing for him—but Estelle sitting on the front passenger seat just had a prime view of his backside which thankfully improved once he was neutered!

New Jwala shareholders from Europe or England who had no experience in 4x4 driving sometimes asked if I could help teach them the tricker aspects of driving the rough reserve roads, negotiating cotton soil mud, deep sand or going down into rocky riverbeds and up steep, rutted banks. Caesar appointed himself chief judge and adjudicator of their skills—or lack thereof. Taking up his position on the flattened windscreen, he made his views abundantly clear. Too bumpy, and he was forced to stand instead of his usual comfortably slouched sitting position. Too sharp on the accelerator or brakes and the brindle head would whip around and the driver got the dreaded *"What DO you think you are doing?"* stare!

Not only did Caesar serve as an excellent driving instructor, but he was also a brilliant snake pointer. Once, when walking near the fire pit at the lodge, he stopped abruptly and peered intently into some low bushes up against the stone seating wall. Taking a stick, I parted the leaf-cover and saw the distinctive V-patterned scales and fat girth of a puff adder, one of southern Africa's most dangerous snakes. Puffies have a lightning-fast strike and potentially fatal cytotoxic venom. They are supposed to have no odour, but Caesar immediately pointed to the hidden snake. Extremely well camouflaged, puff adders are ambush predators, lying motionless until some unsuspecting prey comes scurrying past. But when disturbed or threatened, puff adders at least have the manners to omit a loud and prolonged warning puff or hiss.

While I hooked and remove the puffing snake, I was hugely impressed that Caesar just walked off and ignored the whole procedure. It's a nightmare to try and catch a snake with a hound going berserk, barking and lunging at the already defensive reptile.

He proved his worth again when we were staying in our newly built house at Jwala. It was around midnight so the generator was off, and everything was in darkness. Due to the heat, we slept with the bedroom sliding glass door open but with a concertina-style metal security door stretched across the opening to keep Caesar in and leopards and lions out. This particular night, Caesar woke us by scratching at the mosquito net over our bed. It was something he had never done before, so Estelle lifted the net to see what was wrong. Caesar immediately jumped onto the bed (something he was not allowed to do) and started to 'point' between our pillows.

Grumbling, I got out of bed and picked up a torch. Batteries flat! I went to fetch batteries and once fitted, got down to peer under the bed. I had deliberately built the bed on a recessed base to discourage 'nasties' such as scorpions, armoured crickets and large, really creepy arachnids called 'salifugids', from crawling onto the mattress. But now the gap between the wall and the baseboard was squirming with a very large dark snake. It needed to be identified but I couldn't see its head. A few prods with a Masai spear we had hanging on the wall as a décor item quickly proved this uninvited guest was a cobra, and unfortunately a deadly Mozambique spitting cobra, not only capable of killing with a single bite but also expelling its blinding and disfiguring venom some 2-3 meters at one's eyes with deadly accuracy. So that called for me to find my specs!

The snake must have come in through the open door to look for mice and slithered past Caesar in his dog basket. Caesar woke, warned us, and job done, trotted off to lie in the lounge. Clever boy!

I sent Estelle outside with the torch and told her to shine it through the floor-to-ceiling windows. This allowed me to have two hands free while trying to guide the 2-meter snake out of the doorway. If I went to one side of the bed, it moved to the other. I eventually pulled the mattress off the bed frame, hoping that the cobra wouldn't crawl inside the sheets. It didn't. But the mattress hitting the floor did frighten the snake away from the bed.

Being a glossy tiled floor, this was like a skating rink for the poor cobra as it battled to move off. Often, I could not see where it was in the pitch dark because Estelle couldn't focus the beam of the torch onto it as it slithered around. Adrenalin pumping, I eventually succeeded in manoeuvring it towards the open door using the cow-bell section on the other end of the Masai spear. Trying to keep the bell over its head to avoid being sprayed with venom, we made slow progress. Then I heard a plaintive voice from outside: "Hurry up…I am being attacked by mosquitoes!"

In Estelle's defence, it was a very hot night, and she was stark naked!

Caesar was too intelligent to train. He just knew what to do. If we were travelling from Johannesburg to Botswana and he wanted a pee break, he would stand with his front paws on the centre armrest and look at me. Stop, open the car door, put his lead on and off he would trot to find a suitable spot. Having a thick neck, on occasions his collar would slip off his head. But instead of running off, Caesar would immediately halt, wait for his collar and leash to be put back on, and then continue with his search for an appropriate spot.

Once, when the Limpopo was in flood, we had to enter Botswana through the Martin's Drift, a causeway crossing at a Customs post much further upriver from our normal crossing point— Pont Drift. Although we had the requisite permit from the South African State Vet to allow Caesar into Botswana, we did not have a permit that allowed us to go through the many 'foot and mouth' control points within Botswana. Stopped at the first 'foot and mouth' control boom we were asked by the guard for "permit for dog". We handed the guard the SA permit form which, although unfamiliar to him, he duly examined closely looking for a permit number to write onto his control list.

Fortunately, he spotted a number on the top of the page which satisfied his need. Once our names and the number were inscribed on his list, we dipped our feet in disinfectant (Caesar's included), and were cheerfully waved through, our tyres being sanitised while driving through the disinfecting trough. Only later did we realise that the guard had taken down the miniscule FORM number that one finds on the top of all SA government-issued forms for re-ordering purposes!

While still a pup, if there was water in pools in the Jwala River, Caesar just loved splashing around like a kid. But on one trip, the river was actually flowing! The causeway had dammed the river so the water stretched back some 200 meters towards the lodge. We took a walk down to the concrete causeway to wonder at the sight. The causeway was covered with a shallow flow and Caesar rushed across it and back again in delight. Then he decided to run upstream, thinking that this huge stretch of water was also just inches deep as well. He plunged into deep water. We could see the whites of his eyes as he swam for the very first time. He safely made it back onto the causeway, but it was years before he took another swim! Paddling was great. Swimming, not so much.

Soon after that incident, we were inspecting the water level at the causeway again. The river had stopped flowing and on the downstream side of the causeway, the rock pools were drying up fast. A movement in one of the pools caught my eye. A large barbel was trapped in a small rock pool and would undoubtedly die the next day. Although a credo on most game reserves was not to interfere with nature, I felt the man-made causeway was responsible for the fish's plight. Rushing back to the lodge to fetch a large plastic bag, I returned and lifted the large, whiskered barbel into the bag ready for its relocation to deeper waters back at the lodge.

A screech above my head startled me. Looking up, I saw a juvenile fish eagle perched in a tree next to the causeway, staring down at me with piercing eyes. As the fish would have been too heavy to fly off with, the magnificent, speckled youngster had obviously been looking forward to its demise when it could be eaten in situ. Battling with my conscience, I walked back to the lodge and released the barbel in the waterhole area where it was guaranteed permanent water, and hopefully go on to produce many baby barbels.

Although turning out to be the ideal bush-dog, quiet and not concerned with chasing wildlife, Caesar began to develop a dislike for human headgear—hats, caps and the like. One morning we were having breakfast out on our lapa watching three elephants peacefully browsing under a big Mashatu tree nearby. Caesar suddenly took off towards the path that joined our house to the lodge, barking furiously. Two staff were delivering laundry to us, but in typical Tswana custom, the ladies had balanced the pile of folded sheets and shirts on their heads and were gracefully swaying their way towards our house. Although Caesar knew the ladies well, he obviously did not like the idea of the foreign objects on their heads.

By then his barking had disturbed the elephants and one decided to charge. Thinking it was mock charge, I stayed sitting on the edge of the lapa. But the elephant did not stop! I fled into the house just as she screeched to a halt a mere trunk's length from where I had been sitting. The maids ran back to the lodge, screaming. Caesar looked pleased with himself for having sorted out the trespassing headgear.

Not sure why, but our ugly Staffie/Bull Terrier mix showed no interest in other dogs, with one exception: the Spaniel/Staffie mix on the next-door reserve with whom Estelle had originally fallen in love. That floppy-eared brown softy was the one and only love of Caesar's life.

If she and her owners came for a visit, Caesar was stiff for days afterwards from trying to woo her (despite being neutered!). Even when fast asleep on the back seat of our enclosed Cruiser on the way to Jwala, if her owner's vehicle approached, Caesar would leap out of the window and jump into François' vehicle, looking for his one and only passion! She never reciprocated his interest at all.

One day while resident in our Jwala house, I heard Caesar barking in the direction of the dry Jwala riverbed. As he didn't bark without good reason (like a strange hat on someone's head), I strolled over to the bank and looked down. Not 2 meters below us and less than 5 meters away lay a lioness busy disembowelling a young kudu cow that she had just killed. She looked back at us with a warning snarl that indicated she was not keen to share! I ducked down and retreated as quietly and quickly as possible. But not Caesar. He carried on threatening the lioness from the riverbank.

Once a safe distance away, I began whistling and calling for Caesar. But the barking continued. Eventually, only my starting my Land Cruiser, as if I was leaving, had the desired effect. Caesar came tearing back and jumped into the vehicle, seemingly a lot more afraid of being left behind than being eaten by a lioness. We kept him in the car until we could bring him into a securely closed-up house.

That night we heard the eerie cackling laughter of hyenas and the snarling of the lioness as she tried to defend her kill. Then only the cackling of hyenas. As hyenas are the top predators in the Tuli, the lone lioness must have wisely retreated. In the morning, we tiptoed back to the riverbank and peered over. Much to Caesar's disappointment, there was not a sign of any carcass—not even a fragment of bone nor skin. All that was left was a large area of blood-stained sand and lots and lots of spoor.

Caesar could count. The Jwala manager (or myself in the all too frequent absence of a manager) had to shoot an impala for staff consumption every 10 days. It was a much-valued part of the staff's salary package! Once dispatched, the buck would be dragged to a waiting vehicle and transported back to the lodge. The Cruiser would park under a big tree where a chain and pulley system was used to hoist the animal off the truck for gutting and skinning.

As soon as Caesar heard the rattle of that chain, he sped off to await the meatless, below-the-knee section of the impala's legs as they were severed from the carcass. One by one, the two forelegs and then one hind leg section would be carried back to our house with great pride. But, knowing that hyenas would steal them if Caesar buried them, I would ask him to 'give' each one to me so they could be kept in our Minus 40 chest freezer. Like ice-lolly treats for later. That left the last leg from which the carcass was hanging. Caesar would trot back and wait for leg number four. In the meantime, Albert, the lodge's much-loved driver, would feed him the impala's scrotum and a few other disgusting 'treats'. Once bled-out and skinned, the animal would be apportioned to the staff and only then would Caesar appear home with the last leg. He knew how to count—up to four anyway.

These bones were not allowed in the house, so at night, Caesar reluctantly left his impala leg on his 'futon' outside the huge glass sliding doors that closed off the lounge from the lapa at night. This abandoned leg soon became an easy treat for hyena. At the first sniff of a hyena's presence, Caesar would leap out of his basket in our bedroom and streak down the passageway into the lounge, barking all the way. By the time he reached the lounge, the hyena and the impala leg were gone. But being really smart, our crafty little fellow quickly adopted a new tactic. At the first scent of a hyena, Caesar crept out of his basket and silently tip-toed down the passage towards the unsuspecting thief. Caesar would then launch himself at the glass door barking as furiously as he could. And it worked. The hyena took off and the leg was generally still in place in the morning.

Our boy had no fear of any wildlife. If baboons ventured close to the house, he would see them off with a few seconds of barking. He also terrified us by chasing off hyenas, day or night. But one night he decided to investigate a porcupine. Poor dog arrived at our braai fire with at least 10 quills imbedded in his nose and face. Before we could intervene, he took himself off around the corner of the house and arrived back minutes later without a quill in sight. And he never tangled with a porcupine again.

A nearby reserve had a tame porcupine. Its mother had been killed by lion and the managerial couple had offered to hand-rear the orphaned baby…officially known as a 'porcupette'. At about 6 months old, she became independent, spending her days sleeping around the lodge but venturing out at night. Once fully grown, weighing some 20 kgs and measuring about 80 cms from nose to tail, she still arrived at the lodge most nights for a meal of raw potatoes, apples or dog pellets.

One evening, we were invited for supper and the now fully grown porcupine lumbered into the lapa to join us. Having munched down a potato and two apples, she proceeded to lie down and go to sleep, allowing Estelle and I the rare privilege of stroking a porcupine's belly and feeling her soft padded feet. Caesar ignored her.

Chapter 8
Not for the Faint-Hearted

Some five years into our Jwala shareholding, I had the good fortune to acquire a thatched roof, just a short walk from the lodge.

Some years previously, two shareholders had contracted with a top South African thatching company to partly build two houses in designated spots near the lodge. Foundations were laid and filled with a concrete slab over which thatched roof-structures stood raised up on gum-pole 'legs': a roof and floor but no walls. As fate would have it, both shareholders decided to sell their shares and their 'roof'. I bought one of the roofs.

But building in the bush is not for the faint-hearted.

Having acquired the thatched roof furthest from the lodge and closest to the Jwala River and its waterhole, I spent some time planning the layout of two bedrooms, two bathrooms, open-plan lounge, dining room and huge kitchen. Beyond the kitchen would be a small tool room and finally a large art studio. The house was shaped like a flat-bottomed V. From the bottom of the V, a thatched projection led to our lapa where we ate most meals and, once retired and living there, played Scrabble over lunch. Scrabble was our way of trying to retain some semblance of vocabulary! Living alone in the bush with no careers, no phones and not much by the way of TV or contact with others, meant our conversation was limited to "look at that moon" or "hear that lion?"

While running my company in Johannesburg, I always had two vehicles: a convertible left-hand drive Alpha Romeo for town and a right-hand drive Range Rover for the bush. Having acquired the roof at Jwala, the Range Rover became the building materials delivery 'truck', pulling a 1-ton trailer with high side rails. Over the next two years, I towed up 23 tons of materials; drywall boards, timber, tongue-and-groove planking, a bath, two toilets, sinks, basins, tile cement, paint, plumbing and electrical fittings, furniture, fridges, freezers and kitchen units. Everything. Even all the custom-made floor-to-ceiling glazed windows and sliding doors were towed from Johannesburg to Jwala in that trailer. I bent a crank shaft on one trip and still managed to limp back to Johannesburg.

On another trip, the Range Rover packed up some 10 kilometres from Alldays and the nearest garage. A passing driver agreed to get the Alldays garage mechanic to come and assist us. The said mechanic arrived, took one look at the complexity of the engine, and closed the bonnet! That's when I decided that my next vehicle would be a Toyota Land Cruiser!

However, I towed almost a whole 'house' up to our Jwala site with the Range Rover. Only the required bricks, bags of cement and 220 square meters of tiles were delivered to Jwala by a brave hardware store in Pietersburg. Sand was trucked in from the Limpopo River (when it was not running).

I've described the troubles involved with crossing the Limpopo, and that was in a 4x4 vehicle. A massive truck laden with bricks, cement, floor tiles and such… well, that's a whole new problem. If the truck made it across into Botswana, there was Customs to get through.

I once had to calculate the square footage of all the glass in the doors and windows I was importing in my trailer, plus the length of wood that made up all the frames! I also declared a 2 x 3 metre rug which a Customs official calculated to be 2 square meters and no amount of persuasion from my side would shift him. Oh well, I paid less duty!

Once through Customs, the road leading into the Tuli Block was wide gravel and well maintained, until one took the right-hand turn-off that led north through the Mashatu Game Reserve and other private reserves and finally Jwala, the northern-most reserve in the Tuli Block. That road had never seen a grader. It was mostly just a track that picked its way up hills and down dales avoiding the biggest rocks and softest sand.

Often, if Estelle was off flying, I travelled up to Jwala on my own. One rainy day, with the trailer full of sliding glass doors and floor-to-ceiling-sized windows, I put the Range Rover into low range to cross the Majali River which was flowing yet looked crossable. But when trying to scale the steep, muddy bank on the opposite side, I got stuck. I took a couple of charges at it, but the weight of the trailer sitting in the water and the slipperiness of the steep mud bank resulted in repeated failure. My wheels just spun.

Then, to top it all, two open game-drive vehicles from the world renowned Mashatu Game Reserve, complete with guests clad in matching Mashatu rain-proof ponchos, had now arrived at the bank behind me. I was blocking the only way to their lodge! The rain continued to pelt down as I scrambled up the bank with the winch cable, looking for anything I could fasten it to. A pathetically small bush was all that was available, so, holding thumbs, I hooked the Range Rover's winch to it and slipped down the bank into the car, acutely aware of my every move being watched by 20 pairs of miserable eyes. The bush held and I managed to get up the riverbank and let the Mashatu vehicles pass. I was both embarrassed and elated!

On another trip with the trailer laden with building materials, a game-drive vehicle came roaring up behind us. I stopped. The nice young ranger explained that he had heard on his shortwave radio that "a Range Rover has lost a door". He was intrigued as to how a vehicle could lose a door and the driver not even notice? He gave chase and saw an interior house door lying on the dirt track! Despite all my roping, it had shaken itself off the top of my fully laden trailer! We laughed as he helped me re-rope the slightly dented door back in place.

As the thatched roof of the Jwala house was suspended on a series of gum-poles, it made sense to me that the quickest and cheapest way to build would be to have custom-made windows that fitted between the upright poles and reached from the floor up to the cross-poles that ran across the uprights. I had measured the gap…1.2m wide by 2.38m high. My friend and director in charge of purchasing at my company volunteered to order the ten tall windows, some smaller windows for the kitchen and bathrooms, three standard sliding doors and one massive 4.2m sliding door, the frame of which was to be cut in half on the vertical, so the two halves fitted into the trailer for the trip to the reserve. All the doors and window were fully glazed and took several trips to reach get to Jwala, but amazingly, given the horribly rough, ungraded dirt roads, not one pane of glass broke in transit. (Estelle will not be happy with me mentioning that the only piece of glass to break was at her hands as she varnished one of the window frames.)

Basically, the river side of the house would be glass and the north side, which would be hit by the sun, would be brick inset with smaller windows.

To the chagrin of a couple of Barn owls who had taken a fancy to the roof, building commenced. That's when I discovered that a mistake had been made when ordering. Each window was not 1.2m wide as specified, but 1.12m wide! This proved to be such a fortuitous error as it then transpired that the vertical gum-poles which were going to receive the windows were not exactly vertical! Each one was leaning slightly left or right. So the wrong sized windows fitted beautifully (with some foam filler here and there).

Wildlife did not seem to mind the new house going up. In fact, leguaans regularly took up residence in the roof. These giant lizards (Nile or water monitors) can exceed 2 meters in length and, although harmless when left alone, can open one's flesh with a whipping motion of their tail.

Fortunately, the ones that took to climbing the up-rights into our roof seldom reached a meter long. On removing the first ones I quickly discovered they possess a second and equally effective defence…to empty their bowels of the foulest smelling, black excrement all over their captor!

The biggest problem with building in the bush is that your nearest hardware store is over 200 kms away! On the very first day of building, when fitting a tap to the water pipe laid to the site, I overtightened it and it broke. No spare. No water! A whole day trip to replace a single tap. Good lesson. Buy two of everything, just in case!

Chapter 9
Jim

Having taken a bricklaying course at 18 years of age and extensively modified my last house in Johannesburg (laying every brick, plastering walls and even building the roof myself), I naturally decided that I would build my Jwala house. But I could not do the really heavy stuff like mixing cement, digging a septic tank or cutting the long trench needed to bring water from the tanks to our house.

I spoke to the Jwala staff: four men who did the outside work, maintaining roads, collecting firewood and such, and four women who cleaned and did the laundry and dishes at the lodge. Could they find me someone strong to help me build during my annual leave in November? Employment being so hard to come by in the rural areas outside the Tuli Block, I was confident I would land up with a young, muscular recruit.

Since acquiring the share in Jwala, I always took my annual leave around October/November. Although called 'suicide month' due to the heat, it was also the start of the rainy season which was just thrilling to witness. Great sheets of lightning forked through the night sky, both rare and common flowers burst forth, and the bush looked stunningly clean having been freshly washed of months of dust!

And then, with good rains to the north, there was the possibility that the Jwala River might start flowing again. I can vividly remember the roar of a hundred angels wings that signified the flood water had indeed arrived! After the rains a miracle would occur. Wet riverbanks would be crawling with tick-like mites clad in red velvet. Exquisite white Spider lilies would pop up and die the very next day. And in a week there would be great 'fields' of yellow flowers. Unfortunately these were the dreaded 'Devil's thorn' weeds which left behind hard thorny burrs that were a hazard to bicycle tyres, shoes, bare feet and grazers. Such stunning riches of new life were not to be missed.

So, in the rainy season of 1996, Estelle, Caesar, and I arrived at Jwala to make a start on building our house. On our arrival, the staff had lined up to greet us, singing—a special Jwala tradition—and I eagerly looked for my new helper amongst the familiar smiling faces. At the end of the line was a diminutive, wrinkled old man, so thin he looked like he hadn't eaten for months. He was introduced to me as Jim, my new helper. I was hugely disappointed and sure this poor fellow was not up to the job on hand. It also transpired that we couldn't communicate. Jim spoke several African languages, a touch of Afrikaans, but not a word of English. To my shame, I could only speak English.

Nonetheless, the next day I walked Jim to the water tanks and explained with hand gestures that I needed a trench dug all the way from the water tanks to the slab of the house—some 120-meters. To my amazement by that afternoon, Jim had dug a perfect trench. And once we had laid the pipe, he refilled the trench, even putting back the tall grass he had dug up so there was no sign of any disturbance at all!

Jim became my best building-buddy and my shadow. We did not need language. If I was up on the scaffold and looked around for my spirit level, Jim immediately deduced what it was that I needed and handed it to me. He mixed cement like a wizard and instead of pushing a cement or brick-laden wheelbarrow over the hosepipe, he carefully placed wood off-cuts on either side of the hose so the wheel did not crush the pipe!

On our trips we started to bring gifts for Jim. Once it was a mattress which we dropped off at his hut in his village outside the game area. He refused to take it until he had given us a gift in exchange…a hand-carved, wooden replica of the iconic three-legged cast-iron pots used to cook food over a fire.

After the house was finished, we employed Jim to garden for us and at the lodge. Once we left Jwala, he stayed on…but sadly died shortly afterwards. Jim, my friend, you will never be forgotten.

Chapter 10
Is Your TV On, Madam?

Being a sports fanatic, one of the first things installed in our Jwala house was a TV. I manged to 'bribe' a MultiChoice agent in Mussina (some 200 kilometres away in South Africa) to come and install the dish and a DSTv decoder. Over and above his charge, he was offered a night's accommodation, a steak on the braai and a game-drive. It all went like clockwork. The installer arrived, a satellite dish was bolted high up on an old dead Leadwood right next to the house and the decoder tucked into the TV cabinet. And as the installer was staying overnight, when the generator came on at 6.00pm, he graciously showed us how everything worked. Being a sports fan, I was ecstatic.

But two weeks later, the TV went blank. No DSTv! Early the next morning, I jumped into our old game-drive vehicle and drove through elephants and rivers to get to the border and a phone. As the rains had arrived, I crossed to South Africa on the pont. Inside the large tin shed which served as the arrival and departure platform for the pont, I unlocked Jwala's blue metal truck that was fixed to the shed wall.

In the trunk was the only communication we had with South Africa, a dial-up telephone. For some inexplicable reason, it only worked when the temperature was below $35°$ degrees Celsius. If the roads in Alldays (the nearest village to Pont Drift) were melting in the heat, the line was dead. This meant an early morning trip was essential. (Alldays was reputedly named by nearby farmers who used to arrive at the only pub in the late afternoon and drink until the next morning…thus they had no idea that night had come and gone…it was just daytime…all days!)

Being under tar-melting temperature, I was able to call MultiChoice and was told by customer service that they would activate the decoder immediately.

Happy, I drove back to Jwala through rivers and elephants and at 6.00pm sat waiting for the generator to grunt into life and our TV screen to come alive. It remained ominously black!

Early the next morning, I ventured back through elephants and rivers to make a second call. "Hold on," the lady said. Pause… "is it on now?"

I patiently explained that I could not see the TV as I was an hour away from it, standing in a tin shed on the banks of the Limpopo River and could lose telephone communications any minute if the temperature got too high. Plus the power to the TV would only be put on at 6.00pm. That was going to be a problem as the customer service lady knocked off at 5.00pm but she kindly said that she would leave a note for the night shift team to turn my decoder on just after 6.00pm. Great. Back home I waited for 6.00…6.05…6.10…6.20pm. Decoder still dead. Nothing on the TV. 7.00pm, still nothing.

Morning three and it was a repeat journey. I explained my problem to a new customer service lady starting with the hour-long trip, elephants, the cable-car crossing over the Limpopo River, the phone in a trunk on the banks of the river; everything. "Hold on," she said, "I just have to check something…" Pause… "is your decoder working now?" I totally lost it! Eventually, I was put through to a supervisor, went through the whole story again, and much to my joy we had an active decoder and watched TV that night and onwards!

Sometimes while watching TV, we became aware of eyes looking on through the windows behind us. The staff were fascinated, many had not seen a TV before. Unfortunately, they could not follow the broadcasts due to their somewhat limited English. Trying to find films that they might find easy to follow, I first recorded "The Man-eaters of Tsavo". That was a mistake. Squeezed onto our couches, the ladies shrieked and the men leapt to their feet, loudly shouting out warnings to the actors as the man-eating lions stalked their prey. From that time on, the staff wanted to be driven to the game reserve fence for their days off, too scared to walk!

So, for the next movie, we chose "101 Dalmatians" with Glen Close playing Cruella de Vil. Thinking that it would show them aspects of England—snow, villages, green grassed farms, and such. But it was the animals who could speak and create devious traps for the villains that fascinated our little audience. They left the screening with the firm impression that *English* animals were far more gifted than their African brethren!

Chapter 11
Lion-Proof Lodgings

Like our house, the Jwala Lodge was totally unfenced. In times of drought, the great lawn at the lodge was dotted with warthogs kneeling to graze the green grass. And where there are warthogs there are leopards, hyenas and lion. The lawn was kept green through an underground sprinkler system, and on occasions elephants would come onto the lawn and by putting their trunk-tips over the sprinkler heads, suck the water out of the entire system. But no one really took much heed of the potential danger of having wildlife so close by.

One night a pack of hyenas attacked a lioness just outside the garage area near the manager's cottage. The noise was phenomenal, but the lioness managed to escape.

Once we took up residence at Jwala, each time there was no manager, it became my job to walk through a little forest patch to the lodge to turn on the generator at night. The 6.00pm walk was still light, but the 10pm walk in the pitch black could be a bit nerve-racking. I would listen for sounds such as a lion's roar that might indicate how far (or near) it was. Snapping branches might indicate the presence of elephants. If all seemed quiet, I would walk swiftly across with a flashlight my sole comfort and weapon.

However, lions did not always announce their presence by vocalising. Being so few in number in the Tuli Block and seen as unwelcome rivals by the larger clans of hyenas, a pride of lions could be lying quietly nearby, and you'd never know.

One night Caesar became agitated at something outside the house. Having learnt to respect his warnings, I cautiously opened the top section of the stable-style front door, spotlight in hand. The beam fell on a crouched-over, pig-size grey animal that lumbered off into the long grass and bushes…its elongated snout and droopy

tail gave it away...a rare sighting of an aardvark! Aardvarks are the African version of an anteater. They have sparsely-haired skin, not scales like the pangolin. Despite their size (they can weigh in at 60-80 kg and reaching over 2 meters from snout to tail tip), aardvarks feed almost exclusively on ants. Their sense of smell is reputedly the best of any mammal.

Excited by the opportunity to see more of this visitor, Estelle and I rushed into the dark with spotlights in the hope of catching another glimpse. After some minutes searching, we gave up. Books on animal spoor describe the aardvark as having 5 rear toes but only 4 front toes with sturdy claws for penetrating anthills and digging burrows. So early the next morning off I went to see if I could find any of this distinctive spoor left behind in the sand. Nope. But what I did find was lion spoor—and it was over our own footprints of that night. When had this lion walked past our house? When did it walk over our tracks? Had it been following the aardvark but stopped to watch us bumbling along with our spotlights focused on the ground?

Having established that lions and hyenas were an ever-present threat, I became increasingly concerned for the Jwala staff. They worked on a sort of '3 weeks on, 1 week off' schedule. The accommodation for the time they spent at Jwala was a scattering of tiny wooden huts with a cement block communal kitchen and ablution block to one side. This unfenced 'village' sat on a rise, just a short walk from the lodge near the airstrip. As mentioned, landing strips were prime overnight spots for herds of prey animals, especially wildebeest, as they afforded predators no cover from which to launch a surprise attack. However, overnighting herds did attract hopeful hunters.

In addition to this danger, the meat from the staff's impala rations was cut into strips, salted, and hung on wires between the huts to dry. With no electricity or refrigeration available, the staff used the dried meat strips to cook up as required and seemed to be eaten for lunch, supper, and breakfast. The scent of this meat obviously attracted hyenas and lion at night…and that raised huge concerns for the staff's safety.

Fortunately, the overseas Jwala shareholders were both wealthy and caring! Donations came in and I designed a new 'staff village' consisting of 4 twin-roomed sleeping units with stoeps (verandas) arranged in a semi-circle around a roofed, 'sit and braai' communal area with benches around the fire pit. Just behind this open cooking area was to be an expanded kitchen with two ablution and showering facilities: one for the men on the left and one for the ladies on the right.

And best of all, the whole 'village' would be securely fenced and gated!

The staff were very happy with the plans, except for one aspect. I had included hand basins in the toilet cubicles. After some embarrassed conversation in Setswana, a spokesperson was elected to break the news to me that hand basins must be outside the toilet cubicle. It was commonly held that the Jwala shareholders were quite unclean to have basins in the same room as the toilet! A quick change to the plan and everyone was delighted.

Just two problems. Firstly, the donations stretched to cover materials only…no labour. The staff and I would need to be the builders! Secondly, we needed a brave South African supplier to deliver the materials to what was essentially the middle of nowhere. Indeed, the supplier's truck driver turned out to be a super-hero. He arrived with huge blisters on his gear-changing hand from battling to get across the soft sand of the very dry Limpopo riverbed. Then halfway to Jwala there was a small but steep dip where the track crossed over a stream bed. His extremely long truck got wedge across this mini-ravine like a bridge: front bumper stuck on the up bank and back bumper on the down bank—all wheels off the ground. Fortunately, for the driver and me, another vehicle just happened along and managed to heave the truck forward and get its drive wheels on terra firma again.

Once the truck trundled into the building site laden with some 100 pockets of pockets of cement, hundreds of large pre-cast building blocks, all the roofing timbers, corrugated iron roofing and metal doors and windows, the staff excitedly set about off-loading and stacking these treasures.

Over the next weeks, in staff lunch times and evenings, foundations were pegged, dug out and concrete poured. It was all going very well until the first concrete breezeblocks were laid in preparation for the slabs. That's when I realised that not everyone is a born bricklayer. Despite fishing-line guides dictating where the top and front edge of every block should be, the staff, bless them, seemed to think that being a centimetre off this guideline was not a problem. So, we had to resort to training with wet sand in place of cement until some accuracy was achieved. I could lay with the guys for an hour or two, but then the 20kg breeze blocks got the better of my back and arm muscles. The guys were fantastic and would have carried on all night if left to their own devices.

The huge stack of breezeblocks was slowly shrinking. Much to Caesar's delight the hollow blocks had become a mega mouse hotel. Each day when arriving to build, Caesar would scale the block-pile pushing his snout down every crack and hollow, sniffing for a rat or mouse that might have taken up residence. And when the guys came to take any promising block, Caesar would be standing on it, ready to pounce!

But where there are rodents, there are snakes. Caesar was fortunately 'snake smart' so he stood back if one was inside the block-pile and the grateful staff took note!

After some months of building, the doors and window were in, and the simple mono-pitched roofs were going up. Each staff member was given a choice of paint colour for the inside walls of their rooms. The outside walls were left un-plastered but a visiting salesman keen to recoat the lodge pool gave us a demo of a powder that mixed into a thick, textured, waterproof coating ideal for our needs. A terracotta colour was duly selected and delivered. The village was nearly complete. Just the fire pit area and ablution improvements to go— and that all-important fence. With left-over breezeblocks, we created a short wall that provided the staff with some privacy and in the centre of the wall was a welcoming entrance arch and gate.

I heard from the staff of a large commercial lodge in the area, that Jwala's staff accommodation was the best in the Tuli Block. They had all popped in for a tour!

Unfortunately, my building and teaching skills were put to the test some years after Estelle and I were settled back in South Africa – and failed. I heard that a freak wind ripped the roofs off the staff village leaving devastation in its wake.

Chapter 12
Food Supplies

Many of Jwala's foreign shareholders arranged for an upmarket Johannesburg food emporium to pack their food requirements into polystyrene chests which were duly dropped off at a small Johannesburg airport to be flown up to Jwala on the shareholder's charter plane. South African shareholders just filled trunks and cooler bags with supplies for the week or weekend and drove the five and a half hours from Johannesburg to Pont Drift.

The string of Jwala managers needed to get what supplies they could from Alldays or the rural Botswana villages outside the reserve while on their regular trips to do the banking, draw staff wages and fetch diesel for the generator. They also kindly shopped for the Jwala staff.

Once retired and resident in our Jwala house, Estelle and I shopped once a month in Pietersburg our nearest source of decent foodstuffs some 200 kilometres away in South Africa.

Our shopping days began in a mad scramble to leave at 6.30am to get to the border post in time to be first in the queue when it opened at 8.00am. We then crossed the Limpopo, had our passports stamped on the South African side and were on the tar road for the 2-and-a-half-hour drive to Pietersburg. We had to be back at the South African border post by 3.45pm so that we could get through the Botswana Customs before they closed sharply at 4.00pm. It was dusk by the time we got home.

Being an avid list-maker, I wrote our shopping list in the order of the aisles in the newly opened Pietersburg Mall supermarket. But once the Jwala staff members realised we were planning a shopping day, the list became trickier with items such as bicycle parts, wool, or various medicines tagged on.

Initially we tried leaving Caesar at home. But a kilometre out of the lodge, I spotted a stocky black shape racing behind us in our dust. He would have probably tried to follow us to the border if we hadn't stopped. From then on Caesar accompanied us on our shopping days. In summer that meant Estelle sat with him in the Cruiser with all the windows open while I raced around the shop or shops with the precious list. I must admit to pausing in front of the fruit and vegetable sections just to wonder at the delicious, fresh items on display. In Botswana heat, we were lucky to eat fresh items for a few days…then it was back to tins and frozen foods. And in the 1990's, the variety was certainly not as amazing as it is today.

At 1.30ish came the race back home via a fuel and gas bottle fill-up in Alldays.

Both the South African and Botswanan border posts closed at 4.00pm sharp. If running late, one could phone the SA post and ask them to stay open for another 10 minutes… but the Botswana post had no phone contact, so you might spend the night on the banks of the Limpopo, parked outside their locked gates!

Not everyone has to do a 400-kilometre round trip to do shopping! But that might explain why our kitchen was bigger than most. The open front section facing the dining table and lounge was mostly a 3-metre-long counter complete with a gas stove and even more counters leading to the back scullery section. Hidden behind a wall of tall storage cupboards in the middle were two Minus 40 chest freezers and one Minus 40 fridge. As we only enjoyed generator power four hours a day, the famed Minus 40 brand of specialist farm refrigerators with 20cm thick insulated walls had been the only brand to buy.

"So," you are thinking, "why not grow your own fresh veggies?"

Well, Rodger Petty, the original owner/manager of Jwala certainly tried. He built a sturdy wood-fenced enclosure near to his cottage in which he planted potatoes and various greens. The enclosure kept the warthogs and small buck out…but not elephants or eland. Despite being the world's biggest antelope with bulls weighing over 1,000 kg and measuring some 1.6metres at the shoulder, eland can jump over a car from a standing start! And elephants can make short work of any fencing. So the fence was topped with electric wires powered by a car battery. At night one could hear the occasional burst of trumpeting as an inquisitive elephant got zapped. Then Del, Roger's diminutive wife, used to bravely dash out of her house into the darkness banging a cooking pot to chase the elephants away. But once the battery failed, the elephants took the fence apart!

The next attempt was a growing tunnel: metal half hoops joined together with horizontal metal piping and covered with a strong fencing mesh material. But just as the veggies started to grow, a big bull elephant lifted the whole 12-metre-long tunnel plus foundations clear out of the ground. There was not a plant left. He even helped himself to the small sapling Mashatu trees that Rodger was propagating inside the tunnel with a view to planting them around the lodge when big enough.

Once residing at Jwala, we also tried our hand at growing salad plants—tomatoes, spring onions and lettuce. Estelle tried to cultivate them in large plant-pots placed right at our kitchen door sheltered under the eaves of our house. And just when she was getting excited about a fresh salad, it would all disappear. From the great circular spoor left in the sand, it was obvious that an elephant beat her to it! She tried and tried, but in every attempt, we had elephants in our salad!

We tried every trick in the book. We hung sweaty T-shirts above the pots, sprayed foul-smelling Jeyes Fluid on the pot sides… and still the plants disappeared. We contemplated getting a beehive as elephants are reputedly afraid of bees. Some farmers in Kenya are using lines of beehives instead of fencing to protect their crops from marauding herds. But as we were also afraid of bees, we dropped that idea. To deter elephants from damaging giant baobab trees to get at their water-rich flesh, it is common to ring the massive trees with a 4-meter-wide apron of jagged stones to keep the tuskers away. So, we tried placing sharp rocks around the approach area of the pots. But they just got pushed into the soft sand. We gave up!

Chapter 13
"An Ellie with a Vulture in Its Belly!"

Arriving at Jwala on one of our early 'building' trips, we were met by an excited manager. A somewhat gruff German with a delightful South African wife, Kurt couldn't wait to tell us that in a nearby riverbed there was the carcass of a young elephant with a dead vulture in its belly! He couldn't explain anything more, so Estelle, Jim, Caesar and I jumped into our old open Land Cruiser and followed the spiral of airborne vultures that indicated a meal below.

Parking the game-drive vehicle on the track, we tiptoed through the bush towards the place where the vultures seemed to be landing. (Tip for bush walkers: If the vultures are sitting on a tree…the kill is undoubtedly being consumed by hyenas or lions! If the birds are on the ground…generally safe to approach!)

We could have just followed our noses because the stench was horrible. Soon there was the bizarre sight of a carcass of a young elephant lying on its side. Its underside had been ripped open and its prime organs eaten by leopards or hyena or probably both. Its top ribs formed a cage-like structure.

Young elephants of 5 or 6 years of age are quite vulnerable as after some 2 to 3 years of suckling, their mothers are ready to mate and after a 22-month gestation, a new baby arrives. The older youngster stays with its mother but when it comes to nourishment, it must now fend for itself. In a drought, grass becomes scarce and buck strip the easy to reach lower leaves on bushes and trees making it more difficult for the young elephants to reach sufficient food. Could that explain the calf's demise?

We peered into the empty cavity of the young elephant's core and sure enough there was a vulture inside. Its head was ensnared in loops of now dried gut or sinew in the highest part of the 'cave' and its feet were just touching the bottom floor of ribs. Dried blood coated its feathers. No movement. Jim found a long twig and reaching into the cavity, gave the bird a quick prod. I, staying well away from the stench, was videoing the whole scene, and caught Jim's quick-as-a-flash reaction as the vulture objected to the prod. It was alive!

Now this curiosity had become a rescue mission. Racing back to the lodge, we fetched anything with a long handle that might help free the bird from its prison. Keeping a safe distance was imperative. Vultures can break animal bones to get at the marrow… get too close to the beak and one could lose a finger or two!

Using a knife taped to a long stick, Jim started to free the bird's feet from the web of dry entrails, then set about trying cut its head from its noose of guts. Caesar, who had been intrigued at the start, fortunately lost interest. All we needed was for him to get into the 'cage' to 'help'. After a couple of minutes of cutting and jumping back, Jim had the vulture free. It shuffled out of the carcass, so encrusted with dried blood it was unable to open its wings let alone fly. Lifting its shoulders to stop its caked, folded wings dragging on the ground, it hopped off into the bush looking distinctly undignified and embarrassed but alive.

Glad to escape from the stench, we also headed home quite elated to have saved a life.

Interestingly, The Jwala manager told us that a herd of elephants had plagued the lodge area for about a week before the carcass of the baby elephant had been discovered. The herd was disturbed, restless and aggressive. And then, all of a sudden, it had moved off. Had the family been trying to care for the collapsed youngster and keep predators away?

Over the next days and on subsequent visits to Jwala we kept an eye on the carcass. It slowly disintegrated as leopards, hyenas, jackals, vultures and even warthogs did their jobs. Then came the heart-wrenching sight of branches being placed over the bones…a sign of its herd still mourning its passing. Finally, the skull completely disappeared. No idea why—or what animal chose to take it.

The saying that elephants never forget seems to be true. Skulls of long deceased elephants would often be moved around in the veld and be re-adorned with branches.

Chapter 14
Managing a Bush-Lodge

As mentioned, after the Petty's left Jwala, the reserve was often without a manager. Despite the pay being poor, there was no shortage of adventure-seeking youngsters applying for the job. But the loneliness and isolation soon got them down. Once Estelle and I retired there, I often had to take on the managerial duties for months at a time. Some duties such the day-long trips to Selibe Phikwe (to draw staff wages and buy diesel, lodge cleaning materials, vehicle spares and such), were just boring necessities. I did nearly get arrested on one such trip for driving a vehicle with no doors…but much to my relief, was let off with a warning.

Other duties included collecting shareholders from the border, or ensure their personal vehicle was waiting at the Pont Drift Customs area when they arrived. But by far the worst task was to kill an impala every 10 days for staff rations.

As a child I remember being told that my grandfather had won the King George medal for Bisley shooting in the UK. I was a pretty good shot with a pellet gun but had never shouldered a rifle. The empathetic manager from a neighbouring reserve came to give me some instruction and took me out on my first dreaded 'hunt'. We found a single male and I managed to execute the all-important heart shot. While the guys rushed to the impala to slit the throat (all part of this nightmarish routine), I got back into the vehicle with tears running down my face. I have always been reluctant to harm an insect, let alone kill a beautiful buck.

On our return to the lodge, I must have looked a sight. Being so keen to get the perfect shot, I had got far too close to the telescopic sight and landed up with a substantial cut over my eye from the rifle's recoil. Mixed with tears, the right side of my face was dripping with blood. But being so depressed when arriving home, I wouldn't allow Estelle to clean off the blood and tape the cut closed until much later.

Depression would set in a week before each time the deed was to be done…and lasted until the next hunt. I never got used to the idea of killing an animal and to this day do not understand how people do it for fun!

A few days after this first hunt, I was in the Alldays bouhandel (builders merchant) and got sniggered at by the locals who immediately recognised the bruised and taped forehead as a 'bosveld brandmark'…a 'bushveld brand'. It seems that being too close to the scope and getting clobbered by the recoil is an all-too-common mistake.

The impala hunt was exacerbated by the staff only wanting a big male. Male impalas can weigh up to 75kgs whereas females seldom reach 50kgs. The upside of hunting males is that they tend to be in small bachelor groups of two or three where females, especially in rutting season would congregate in herds of 50 or 100 or more, guarded by a single male determined to mate with them all. Obviously, one would never shoot near such a gathering. The ideal is to find a large lone male.

On a trip back from the border one day, there standing alone right on the side of the road was a magnificent male impala. He was huge. And he just stood there ignoring me. *What a pity I don't have a gun with me now,* I thought. Then I realised that I did! The rifle was behind my seat. And as that realisation hit me, the impala took off with a sudden leap and raced off. This incident served to confirm my belief in human/animal communications!

Chapter 15
Harry and Sally

Once living in our finished house, we made some unexpected friends. Caesar's water bowl was situated in the lounge. Every night a toad suddenly appeared in the bowl and quietly floated there for hours. No croaking—ever—and not a trace of him/her when we searched our house in the mornings. One night I mentioned to Estelle that the toad had "sallied forth" so from that time he/she was named Sally.

Generally, Estelle and I were on our ownsome. And when one lives such an isolated life (yes, there was the Botswana staff and the occasional shareholder visit plus often-times a managerial couple), one tends to lose one's vocabulary. Watching TV when the generator was running did help, but our real fix was to play two games of Scrabble every lunchtime.

Our Botswana staff had a two-hour lunch break due to the intense noontime heat. So, we followed suit and sat in the shade of our thatched lapa and unpacked the Scrabble set. During these lunchtime games we noticed a huge lone eland hanging around our house.

Eland are magnificent antelope but notoriously shy. If one comes across a herd of fifty or more while driving in the bush, they generally can't be seen for dust as they rapidly trot off through the bush. They can reach speeds of 40 kph at a full run. Elands all have a slight hump at the shoulders and prominent dewlap. The straight, sharply pointed, horns of both sexes slant backwards with a tight spiral at the base. Horns of as much as one metre in length have been recorded. Eland, I am told, are being farmed for meat in Russia, as they put on weight faster than cattle and on less feed.

Males have a patch of dark hair on their foreheads that covers glandular skin. Our male also had a thick mat of ginger hair, like a long-bristled doormat draped over his neck. Where eland usually have fawn coloured coats with very faint vertical white stripes on their sides, our visitor was a handsome silver grey indicating his advanced age.

Soon this lone eland took to joining us every lunchtime, lying in the shade of trees some 10 paces away. Just resting and chewing his cud. We called him Harry…although this Harry never met Sally.

We had no idea why Harry was alone nor why he adopted us. But in the three plus years that we lunched together he never developed a liking for Caesar. If he spotted Caesar, Harry would lower his great head until his thick twisted horns were parallel to the ground and he would charge. Caesar quickly scooted out of the way, but the trouble was that Caesar was always with me or Estelle, so we had to get out of Harry's way too!

One of my favourite video clips is of Harry locking his great horns into the branches of a Mopani tree just meters from our lapa. He tugs downwards to break the branches so he could browse on the green, butterfly-shaped leaves. But our bird/squirrel feeding plank was hanging from that same branch. Suddenly, Estelle rushes pass me shouting "F**k OFF, HARRY! HARRY, STOP THAT!" … and amazingly, he did!

Chapter 16
Elephant Encounters

Elephants frequently came to the lodge swimming pool to drink. On one occasion when I got too close with my video camera, I was charged by a tuskless matriarch and was forced to beat a hasty retreat under the lapa roof. She slapped her trunk over the low wall surrounding the fire pit, smelling for me. Perhaps she was thinking of ripping away the thatch roof to get at the presumptuous intruder. After a few snorts of disgust, she fortunately marched off with her head held high, back arched with her herd on her heels.

But that was just the beginning of my close encounters with these great and fascinating beasts.

Early in our love affair with Jwala and before building our house, Estelle, Caesar and I would stay in the lodge accommodation. As the lodge was for shareholders and their guests only, there was usually accommodation available and on one visit, the 'honeymoon' rondavel was free, so we slept there. The door was almost hidden by a luscious hibiscus bush resplendent with glorious pink flowers. At about midnight I woke to the sound of the hibiscus being devoured. From the window I could see the huge grey shape of an elephant. Determined to save the hibiscus bush, I opened the door a crack and shouted. Shocked, the elephant backed off. But 6-month-old Caesar obviously believed that as I had chased the animal off, it was his job to do so too!

Like a flash he shot past my legs into the pitch black (remember the generator was always turned off at 10pm) and he pursued the elephant yapping as loudly as he could. Perhaps the 6,000kg pachyderm caught a glimpse of the 6kg puppy and decided that this impertinence was not to be tolerated, for it wheeled about, trumpeted, and gave chase. Estelle lay in bed paralysed with fear for her puppy while I stood in the door fearing the worse. We were both hugely relieved when Caesar bolted back into the room between my legs. But, before I could close the door, he skidded to a halt and dashed out again, yapping furiously! This time the elephant must have taken him seriously as in the morning we could see massive muddy elephant footprints between the lapa and boma and all the way down the slasto path, past the various lodge rooms, past the manager's cottage and generator room, and out towards the safety of the bush!

From that time onwards, Caesar decided that elephants were just a bunch a of sissies. When we heard water splashing at the water hole signalling that a herd of eles had arrived at the water hole to drink and enjoy a mud-bath, we would tiptoe over to the rustic hide perched high up on the riverbank as it afforded a great view of the wildlife enjoying the water. After a while, Caesar would get bored and nonchalantly get up from our feet and wander out of the hide. The next thing, we would see him cooling off in the water hole with elephants on either side of him. Provide he kept quiet, the herds tolerated this strange black, overweight-jackal-looking animal in their midst.

Every morning and every evening, Estelle and I walked in the bush. Caesar took to walking some 20 meters in front of us. If he saw game such as giraffe, buck or zebra, he would stop and turn to look at us. If we stopped, he stopped. If we walked on, he walked on. There were only three exceptions: lion, hyena… and elephants.

If he picked up the fresh scent of lion, he would just sit and walk no further. No amount of calling would shift him. Not understanding what his problem was, we usually turned around and Caesar would happily trot back to the lodge 20 paces ahead of us as usual. I once tested his refusal and decided to carry on walking. That's when I saw the flicking of a lioness's tail behind a fallen Leadwood tree. I retreated very quietly and never doubted Caesar's lion-scenting ability again. On the occasions that I found lion spoor next to the water hole, Caesar would happily follow it with me. I took this as a clear indication that the pride was long gone.

If he scented hyena, the foremost predator in the Tuli area, he just took off and chased them! Day or night. Hardly daring to breathe, we would wait for the sound of his two brass ID discs clinking together to verify that he had survived his idiocy and was on his way back. A female spotted hyena weighs some 60 kilograms and measure 80-90 centimetres at the shoulder. Fully grown, Caesar weighed about 20 kg at best!

But due to his puppyhood experience of successfully chasing an elephant, these giants topped his list of exceptions. If he saw/smelled/heard elephants, he just kept on walking! And we would suddenly find ourselves on foot in the middle of a herd!

We often had to quietly tiptoe out of the middle of a herd. Backwards!

The owner of a reserve in the Tuli Block had been walking with his daughter when they found themselves amongst elephants. A young bull decided to mock charge the pair. A mock charge is signified by ears being spread out wide and the trunk extended. If it's a serious charge, the ears are flat against the elephant's head and the trunk curled between its tusks. Bellowing noises accompany either threat. The two walkers dropped to the ground and curled into tight balls, arms protecting their heads. Confused, the young bull stopped. The herd then circled the pair investigating them with their trunks and even nudging them with their massive feet - but doing no harm. The herd then wandered off!

It beggars belief, but these massive pachyderms can be hard to see when you are walking. They can disappear behind the bushes and be absolutely silent. The footpad of an elephant is made up of a thick spongey substance that absorbs the massive weight of the animal. When a human steps on a twig or dead branch it will make a sharp cracking noise, but not so with an elephant. Its great footpad just muffles any tell-tale 'crack', so they move unbelievably silently. The only give away is the very occasional deep 'tummy rumble' used to communicate, and the occasional breaking of branches if feeding.

One summer's day, a matriarch had led her herd to the Jwala swimming pool for a drink. I began to video the great grey bodies calmly quetching their thirst, using their trunks to deposit water into their mouths. I loved the view of their wrinkled bums, especially when they moved their weight onto one back leg and casually crossed the other in front of it, like guys lounging at a bar! I was busy videoing a youngster who had discovered a hosepipe still connected to a tap near the pool. All outside taps had to be enclosed in a brick and mortar 'box' to protected them from ellies tearing them off to get at the water. This hosepipe should not have been left exposed and it was now being shaken and tugged at with great enthusiasm by a playful 3-4 year-old.

But suddenly my attention was seized by a frightening scream. The herd's matriarch was flapping her great, veined ears, and kneeling at the pool's edge on her front legs to reach her trunk as far as possible into the pool. Still screaming, she got back on her feet and rushed to the shallow end of the pool, decimating a large succulent bush that was in her way. She then began sucking up gallons of water in her trunk and expelling it onto the ground with force as if trying to empty the pool. And that is when I noticed a tiny, black, snake-like object rising from the water. Her baby had fallen into the pool! The 'snake' was its trunk waving above the water enabling it to breathe. Unlike Mpho at the start of this book, this baby was desperate to get out. Down on her front knees again, mom wrapped her trunk around her baby's body and helped it mount the steps and onto dry land.

What intrigued me was mom's reaction. Once she was sure that her baby was safe, she walked away from the pool with her head held very high and her back arched. She then swung around and bellowed at the pool as if to say—*"don't you EVER try that again!"* The herd then quickly disappeared into the bush.

We had several scrapes with a tuskless matriarch that seemed to like Jwala. The road that led to the lodge was a semi-circular curve and one evening this huge female was standing with her small herd in what would have been the centre of the circle. I don't know what annoyed her, but as soon as our game-viewing vehicle took that road, she began to threaten us. Ears flapping and trunk flaying she trumpeted for us to move off. But because the road was a curve with her in the centre, I simply couldn't get any distance away from her. Anxiously I 'put foot' and we sped into the garage area of the lodge where there was fortunately just enough space for the vehicle to slide in. The matriarch followed us right to the garage but fortunately managed to stop before crashing into the line-up of expensive 4 x 4s!

A more dramatic encounter occurred some years later when I had retired and Estelle, Caesar, and Lucky (our cat) had moved into our Jwala home.

While out on an evening walk, we encountered a herd of some twenty elephants moving towards the waterhole at the lodge. I indicated to Estelle that we should make a move to a hillock nearby that might afford us some invisibility if we could hunker down behind it, out of sight. But the wind was swirling around, and the herd caught our scent. The beasts stopped in their tracks, trunks raised smelling the air. The younger elephants became more and more disturbed, milling around, trumpeting, flapping their ears and making mock charges towards us. There wasn't a tree in sight, just Mopani bushes. At one stage I glanced around to see where Estelle was only to see she was halfway up a Mopani bush, her feet about a meter from the ground. Had an elephant carried out a charge, Estelle's body was at the most convenient tusk-goring height! Persuading Estelle down, we crested the hillock—only to find a second herd was making its way to the water hole on that side of the rise. We were in the middle of an elephant sandwich!

I pocketed Caesar's collar with its clicking brass ID tags, and as silently as possible we crept down the far side of the hillock as both herds were wanting to get to the waterhole at the lodge.

Although this route took us away from the lodge, I believed it to be the safest plan given that now both herds were upset by our scent.

After about a kilometre, we came to a shallow, dry streambed with some large trees on its banks. Estelle clambered onto my back to reach the lower branches of a tall Appelblaar tree and managed to climb her way up to 'higher than elephant' level; very brave given her fear of heights!

It was now almost dusk. Caesar and I took off at a lope looking out for the dirt track that would lead us back to the lodge and a vehicle. Found the track. No sound of elephants. Made it home just after sunset, grabbed the keys and leapt into our closed Land Cruiser and headed back to…where?

I only had a vague idea as to where I had left Estelle! Turning off the track, I off-roaded towards the streambed and soon tall trees greeted my headlights. I parked and stupidly turned off the engine which automatically turned off the lights. Now the dilemma… should I walk left, upstream, or right, downstream? I chose right. The sun had disappeared some while ago but typical of Botswana, the horizon was still glowing an awe-inspiring orange. Suddenly, I saw Estelle's silhouette in the distance. But she was climbing further up the tree. Why up? Had a herd of elephants turned back and was now underneath her?

As there was no sound of angry trumpeting, I ventured closer. Not an elephant in sight. Estelle clambered down to earth via my back, allowing me to inquire as to why she had ventured further up the tree. She proudly held up her luminous green bikini top.

She had hung it on a high branch to help me find her, and once she spotted my vehicle's lights, she had gone up to fetch it. A tiny bikini top… in miles and miles of bush. Lucky her silhouette was considerably bigger!

Laughing, we started to make our way back to the vehicle in the dark. Caesar had been trained (or perhaps more accurately had decided it was his job, to always be able to *find the car*), and cleverly led us to the big white Cruiser in the dark. Soon we were bush-whacking our way back to the dirt road and home. Trouble was, unbeknown to us, the first herd of elephants had now arrived in our path. At one stage, I unwittingly drove so close to an elephant my side window went quite black. Gulp.

When we reached home, my mouth was so incredibly parched from the running and rush of adrenalin that I just managed to croak to Estelle, "Do you want some water?"

"No," she replied, "I want something MUCH stronger!"

Later that night, while sitting outside next to our braai fire, a herd of elephants walked past us like great silent ghosts. Estelle was so happily relaxed on port, I thought she was going to invite them to join us.

Chapter 17
Fireside Tales

On their visits to the Jwala, shareholders inevitably ended the day sitting on the huge circular stone bench around the fire, talking, while dinner sizzed over glowing red-hot coals. (Braaing, the South African version of a barbeque, is a favourite pastime in South African homes and although I had often braaied before becoming a shareholder, I embraced the opportunity of learning the finer art of cooking over coals from Rodger Petty. The fire is made of old, hard, dried wood and once the flames have died down to glowing embers, a portion of these coals are spread out quite thinly under the cooking grid. The balance is heaped to the side to form a 'nursery fire' and used to add to the cooking coals as and when extra heat is needed.)

Add beers, brandy or wine to this recipe for a perfect bushveld evening and some great tales emerged.

Rodger once recounted the tale of a bunch of lads staying at the lodge who had been boasting of being confronted by elephants, leopards and lions and were only alive to tell such tales due to their great courage and bravado. Later that night, asleep in their rooms with windows open and mosquito nets over their beds, the stillness was broken by a bloodcurdling yell for help! "Get it off me…leopard!…HELP!" Armed with torches, the guys bravely rushed to their mate's rescue and found him fighting off Roger's pet cat! It had jumped through the window to enjoy the night on a bed but was now entangled in the mosquito net, desperately trying to escape its suddenly not-so-heroic host!

One of our overseas shareholders told us this story around the fire one night: he had decided to fly to Botswana with his son, hire a 4 x 4 vehicle and tent, and drive from Maun to Jwala so that they could see more of the country. Come nightfall, they pitched their tent near the road in the middle of nowhere. (There is a whole heap of 'nowhere' in Botswana…it is the 48th largest country in the world, about the size of France…yet the population is less than 3 million!)

In the early hours, father and son heard rasping noises on the tent sides, like creatures trying to tear their way through the fabric. It was still dark, but they could see the canvas sides being pushed inwards and all about. Terrified, they tried to imagine what strange African animals might be attempting to get to them. The assault was relentless and on all four sides of the tent. At dawn, the shareholder cautiously unzipped the tent entrance to see what on earth could be so persistently attacking the tent. A great grey tongue blocked his view, but when it withdrew, it revealed a small gathering of thirsty Botswana cattle enthusiastically licking off the dew that had accumulated on the tent fabric!

Estelle and I invited a new overseas shareholder to join us for supper on their first evening at Jwala. Christopher and his wife Elaine were delightful, and chatting was easy. Christopher suggested we get to know each other better by telling what he termed 'knock-on' stories. He would start by telling a tale about themselves then Estelle and I would then recount a story about ourselves, and so on.

His tale went like this: as a young man, Christopher had been at university in England when he met a beautiful English girl. The relationship soon became serious enough to warrant her accompanying him to the family home in Switzerland to meet his parents. As was the custom in those days of yore, the couple were shown to two different bedrooms. In the morning, as they met in the passageway on their way to breakfast, Christopher slipped a piece of paper into Elaine's hand.

She took up the story: it was a used envelope…and on the back was a handwritten list of some ten attributes including 'make a good mother', 'well-spoken' and 'intelligent'. Next to each attribute was a score: 6 or 8 or 5 and so on. The scores had been totalled to 68 out of 100 and next to the total were the words 'marriageable proposition'.

Elaine was puzzled. Later that day Christopher asked her what she thought. "About what?" she asked.

"About my marriage proposal," came the answer. They had been happily married for some 30 years when we were told this story. At least Elaine knew in advance that she was marrying the most unromantic of men! Having listened to this tale, I could not think of one story to top theirs, so the knock-on stories started and ended with Christopher's one-of-a-kind proposal!

One of my best bush stories was related by a client of mine; an extremely attractive lady who had been swept off her feet by a bush-loving fellow who was now insisting they spend a weekend away in the bush. Although daunted by the idea, she agreed but made it clear that squatting over a hole to do her 'thing' was something she was not happy to do! Come the dreaded weekend and as her suitor unpacked his bakkie deep in the bushveld, she was presented with a genius gift. Her partner had revamped a folding camp-chair by removing the seat canvas and bolting a toilet seat in its place! This was soon set up over a nice hole away from the tent behind a thick clump of bushes. She was delighted.

The next morning, while my client was 'enthroned' on this gift, panties and shorts down at her ankles, to her absolute horror, a group of birders suddenly emerged from the bush! Surprised to see a camper sitting on a deck-chair in the middle of nowhere, they started up a conversation. What birds had she seen? Wasn't the moon glorious last night? And so on. Fortunately, they seemed not to notice the hole under the chair, nor the fact that her legs were bare and that her face was a red as a tomato!

Chapter 18
Of Guests and Visitors

Owning a share in a game reserve made me instantly more popular with friends, family, clients and my company staff members.

One of my favourite clients was a fabulous lady of colour. In her youth, she had fallen in love with a white man during those dreaded apartheid years when interracial mixing was illegal in South Africa. They escaped jail by fleeing to England where they married, and she rose up the ranks in the burgeoning new cell-phone industry. Years later, she was brought back to South Africa to head up marketing for a new mobile phone company here. By then, the couple had a beautiful little girl. They were delighted to join us one Christmas and we decorated a dried-out aloe flower-stem as a Christmas tree.

But the highlight of the weekend was their toddler's glee in hearing the word 'impala' for the first time. She amused us for the rest of the holiday by pronouncing impala in what seemed like 20 different ways by placing the emphasis on a different letter each time: Impala… iMMpala… imPala… impalA… impaLa… impAla…!

On another occasion, I hosted two company directors (clients). Both had seemed as serious as a heart attack in a work environment, but one afternoon we had stopped to wander around an area rich in agates and quartz crystals that gleamed across baren patches of soil. When they clambered back into the game-drive vehicle, their shorts pockets were bulging with stones. These worthless treasures brought out a childlike joy in these men made obvious by the chatter behind me: "Look at this one", "Ah, but look at THIS one", "And this agate has such distinct bands", "I see yours has more bands, but mine is bigger." A trip to the African bush creates a sense of awe and childlike wonder in even the most hardened souls!

On a couple of occasions, I invited groups of Paton Tupper staff. On one such weekend, while returning from a game-drive at night, my trusty old game-drive vehicle came to a shuddering halt and refused to resume duty. It was pitch dark, no moon and the spotlight had died in sympathy with the vehicle engine. Traditionally one carried a handheld radio for such events, but as there was no manager at the time and no one else at the lodge, I had not taken the radio. "Now what?" came a tremulous voice from behind me.

"No problem," I heard Estelle pipe up, "Chris will walk to the lodge and fetch another vehicle!"

So, duly appointed saviour of the group and with a great degree of trepidation, I alighted from the Cruiser and, accompanied by Caesar, we walked off into total blackness. The lodge was about a kilometre away. Lion and elephants were my main concern, and leopards might be eyeing Caesar with delight. All such predators frequented the area at night due to the nearby waterhole. But seeing Caesar's delight at an unexpected walk, I relaxed a bit. He would warn me if leopard or lion were present…or would he? Anyhow, we reached the lodge without incident and rescued the stranded party without any loss of life!

My company always did pro bono work for charities. One such cause was the performing Lipizzaner horses in Johannesburg; then the only recognised school in the world outside Austria which trained Lipizzaner horses in the style of the famous Spanish Riding School in Vienna. Being an avid animal lover, I often went to see these magnificent white stallions perform their intricate dances and unique leaps. At one such performance there was an appeal for funds. I volunteered the services of one of my most talented artists, Julian Myburg, who drew outstanding portraits of four of the school's Lipizzaner stallions. Framed prints were then sold to Lipizzaner fans and corporations. Some of the funds raised would help bring a retired Spanish Riding School trainer from Austria to South Africa to enhance our riders already breathtaking skills. And to sweeten the deal he and his wife were invited to spend a couple of days at Jwala. 'A unique African experience'. And unique it turned out to be!

I met the couple a few days before the trip to brief them on what to pack and find out what they did or did not eat. That is when I discovered that Helmut only spoke German. Fortunately, his wife, Heidi, could understand a little English. Haltingly, so Heidi could attempt to translate, I explained what the trip was about, and as all our food and drink would be coming up in the same vehicle, they should please pack light. To my amazement, on arriving at dawn to fetch the couple, they stood waiting—both immaculately dressed, from hats to shoes, in white! Slight misunderstanding of the term 'light', I guessed. Anyway, off we set with Caesar proving to be all that Helmut needed to enjoy the five-hour drive to Botswana. And Caesar willingly accepted all his attention.

As you might have gathered, it seldom rains in the Tuli area, but as luck would have it, on that day as we approached Pietersburg, the sky was ominously purple. We stopped in the town and Estelle quickly scurried from shop to shop trying to procure some raincoats. Nothing! She did manage to purchase one umbrella and so we continued north into the gathering gloom. Sure enough, just before the border, we hit rain. I warned Heidi that the vehicle waiting for us in Botswana had no roof. We could not continue in the

Range Rover because the Limpopo River was too deep to cross. She translated for Helmut and neither seemed at all concerned about a good soaking.

Once through SA Customs, we offloaded our luggage and food supplies into the pont and were soon swaying our way across the sand-coloured waters of the Limpopo. Caesar was an old hand at such crossings, but Helmut cradled him safely anyway. Once everyone cleared Botswana Customs, I trotted up the road to fetch the old roofless Jwala Land Cruiser that was standing in the rain.

First problem: the old, very used driver's seat had long been ripped along the centre stitching, and as I plonked myself down behind the wheel, water gushed up between my legs. Embarrassingly, my khaki shorts now looked for all the world like I had peed in my pants!

Second problem: the windscreen was predictably folded down over the bonnet. But as an old hand at such things, I was sure that the fixing bolts needed to secure it upright would be in the glove compartment. But they were not. So, once we were all on board, I had to ask poor Helmut to sit in the front passenger seat and hold the windscreen upright. More embarrassment!

Estelle, ever ingenious, tied an almost waterproof canvas sheet from the top of the windscreen and over Helmut's and my heads so that she and Heidi, sitting on the raised bench behind us, could hold the other end up against their shoulders for protection. But as the drive progressed, rainwater pooled around my and Helmut's heads like large watery haloes. Whenever the vehicle jolted over the rough and rocky road, these rainwater pools landed up spilling all over Estelle and Heidi behind us. Fortunately, the sky cleared before we reached Jwala and the cloth was no longer required. And thanks to the typical Botswana heat, we arrived almost dry.

But then a third problem became apparent. The rains had fallen in South Africa and southern Botswana and were moving north. So, all the game in the Tuli Block had vanished. This is a typical happening… as soon as there are good rains, the animals migrate towards the heaviest rainfall areas to enjoy better grazing and browsing. Never had I driven from the border to Jwala without seeing at least 100 animals. But this time, with these important guests on board, not a whisker nor the flick of an ear behind a bush. The next day was the same. Just a single sighting of a solitary steenbok. This dwarf antelope is one of the smallest in Africa and although very cute, it was not exactly an impressive sighting.

That afternoon, leaving Helmut happily by the pool, I tried driving to a different section of the reserve with Heidi, Estelle and Caesar in the hope of finding elephant, zebra, wildebeest… anything. But instead, I managed to get the vehicle stuck in mud, and not any old mud…this was cotton soil. Cotton soil, given water, fluffs up like heavy, black, sticky cotton-candy. I jumped out of the vehicle to collect dead branches to shove under the wheels for traction. And bless her heart, Heidi joined in…dressed in her pure white Nikes and spotless white dress. Caesar had also jumped out, and once the requisite branches were in place, we were ready to try and escape the mire. But before Heidi could get back into the passenger seat, Caesar jumped onto her seat and then onto his position on the flattened windscreen, paws caked in black mud. Heidi's seat was a horrible black mess. She squelched back to the vehicle with her new white Nikes transformed into massive black Minnie Mouse-like shoes and gamely sat down!

But all was not lost. That night, cooking supper over glowing coals, I heard the familiar grunting call of a lioness not too far away. Twenty minutes later and her roar was much closer. Sure enough, she was heading our way and would very probably make her way to the air strip in the hope of finding impala or wildebeest taking advantage of the clearing. "Quick," I said to our guests, "come…we will drive onto the landing strip so at least you can see a lion!"

Our guests talked between themselves and the answer from Heidi was a very definite "No! Thank you…in Austria, vee haff only foxes!" she explained. The idea of confronting a lion at night in an open vehicle with no doors did not appeal to the couple at all.

The next day, I spotted spoor on the muddy track. I signalled to Helmut to join me on the road so at the very least he had seen proof of leopard being around. He was about to swing himself off the vehicle when a sharp "Helmut, NEIN!" came from the rear of the vehicle and Helmut smartly returned to his seat. The couple must have enjoyed themselves though, as some weeks later, a mysterious small wooden box arrived at the Alldays post office for us. It held a delicious chocolate-covered tort all the way from Austria. Enclosed was a touching thank-you note saying how much they had enjoyed the trip.

A friend once asked if she could possibly bring her mom and stepdad to Jwala. What a pleasure. Estelle and I duly arrived at Pont Drift to collect them. What my friend had neglected to say was her stepdad was 80 years old and somewhat frail. He was unable to climb the stepladder to access the rear game-viewing seats, so he sat next to me in the front. Luggage loaded and off we set. After some minutes, I spotted a small group of giraffes so stopped for the party to admire their grace and beauty.

Out of the corner of my eye, I saw Max scribble something in a tiny notebook and then look at his watch. Assuming the watch-checking signified that he had had enough of watching giraffe and was now bored, I carried on. But whatever animals we stopped to look at, my companion would write in his little book and then look at his watch… so I would move on again. This was the pattern for the rest of the weekend. Later it was revealed that this was not a signal that he was bored. Just the opposite. This little old man was a compulsive diarist. All his interesting life had been inscribed in tiny notebooks. A whole room of them. Every event and its time were noted, but all in a private code of his own invention. He unfortunately died a few years later, leaving a room full of memoirs but no clue as to how to decode them!

Some good friends in Johannesburg were somewhat less happy to venture into the 'wild'. But armed with malaria tablets and Christian faith, they came. Estelle and I moved into the spare room so that Vicki and Toni could enjoy the view from our almost-all-glass bedroom.

I had built a small cement pond close to the house the shallows of which was enjoyed by a host of bathing birds and the deeper section became a popular cooling-off spot for a family of warthogs. But our favourite view was of the porcupines that came to collect a scattering of Caesar's dog pellets that we tossed out of our bedroom window most nights. I had rigged up a solar-powered, motion-triggered light so we could enjoy the porcupines' visits or any passing game. Being solar-powered, the light was set to stay on for just a few seconds so as not to drain the battery.

Having briefed our friends to look out for the porcupines, we all retired to bed. Toni, being a light sleeper was woken by the soft click of the light being triggered and saw a huge porcupine tucking into the dog food right outside the floor-to-ceiling windows. She quickly shook Vicki awake…and the light went out! This happened several times, but Vicki never woke in time to see the splendid animal resplendent in its long black and white banded quills.

One pair of businesswomen friends were particularly delightful. Leolyn had a hugely inquisitive mind. While on a game drive we passed a small Mopani shrub and there, perched in its lower branches about 3 feet off the ground, was a large, dry, elephant dropping. Nearly the size of a football, it did look somewhat incongruous. For the next hour of driving, Le conjured up perhaps 20 explanations as to how the dropping might have got there… could the shrub grown and in doing so lifted the dung skywards with it? … could a strong whirlwind have picked it up and lodged it in the bush? … perhaps a baby ellie had been playing with it like a ball and tossed it into the tree? Eventually we agreed that the explanation where an elephant had backed into the bush and deposited it there while browsing on another Mopani nearby was perhaps the most feasible. Why this particular drive is so memorable was the fact that most newcomers to a game drive experience are usually totally focused on seeing game…not wondering about the other fascinating aspects of the bush itself.

During Le and Re's stay (they had come along with Vicki and Toni of the "*wake up…Porcupines!*" debacle), Estelle and I decided to show off a Botswana sunset from a hillock on an adjoining reserve in which we also had a share. The hillock had been hilariously christened 'Swiss Peak' by the Swiss shareholders. No road led to the base of the hillock so I parked as near as possible and we walked the last kilometre through the bush, Caesar in the lead. On the way I mentioned to our guests that elephants 'might' be on the far side of the hillock as we had seen plenty of droppings there previously. As we walked, I kept glancing at the rapidly setting sun and decided we really needed to pick up the pace or we would miss the sunset from the 'peak'. Unbeknown to me, our guests concluded that the fast pace indicated that we were being pursued by something dangerous! Despite being unused to the relentless heat and the demands of climbing a steep incline, they scrambled upwards close on my heels. Only after admiring the peaceful sunset view complete with giraffes in the distance, did they confess to have been convinced that we had been in grave danger of being eaten by lions or trampled by elephants on the way up. Strangely, we did find smallish elephant droppings and spoor right at the top of that steep, pyramid shaped hill. Must have been left by some adventurous young ellies playing hide and seek?

I had good but 'very British' upbringing. Terribly polite, no hugging, and not much parent/child interaction. So I was overwhelmed by another set of visitors. We had invited two friends to visit the reserve and they asked if they could bring a sister and her two children, plus the sister's best friend, her hubby and their two children. Okay. Bear in mind we had no cell phones in those days, so it came as a bit of a shock when we met the party at the border only to learn that our two friends had taken ill and couldn't be there! Here we were, meeting a whole bunch of strangers. But they proved to be fabulous people, so the weekend went very well.

The most memorable part of their stay was during the late afternoon of their penultimate day. The sun was going down in a magnificent orange sky, the tall yellow grasses between the lodge lawn and the dry riverbed were glowing, and everything was still. And then the sister's friend walked across the lawn followed by a string of four children. They all disappeared into the tall grass. Absolute silence. I was intrigued. About an hour later, they returned. Over supper, I asked the mother of two of the children what this excursion had been about. She explained that she had told the kids to bring notebooks and go sit alone in the bush and write down what they *felt*! I was stunned. My folks never asked me what I *FELT*. Did yours? Bet those kids are married now and raising splendidly balanced children who are all able to express their deepest feelings!

Chapter 19
Day and Night

While we were new to Jwala, Estelle was always worried that in driving around its 5 100 hectares, we would get horribly lost and even land up in Zimbabwe. Being extremely flat, there were few opportunities to get to a lookout point to see where we were, so having a map in your mind and keeping an eye on the sun was essential.

Most of roads were only tyre tracks wending through the bush. And in a good rainfall year, if some tracks were not driven on, the tall grasses just took over and the road disappeared. One would then have to get out of the vehicle and try and look for signs of the track on foot.

But at night everything becomes a whole lot more difficult. All one can see is whatever is illuminated by the headlights or a handheld spotlight. Night drives are popular though. The beam of the spotlight can pick up the reflection of a hundred impala eyes like gleaming stars. Eyeshine in animals is produced by a special membrane, called the *tapetum lucidum* ("tapestry of light"), a reflective surface located directly behind the retina. At night, when starlight or moonlight enter the animal's eye, it reflects off the membrane, giving the eye a second boost of light. For animals that have this membrane, it is like having a built-in flashlight that lights a path from the inside out. Some eyeshines are red, some green, but mostly white. (Humans don't have a tapetum lucidum so we do not see well at night — and when our eyes appear red in photographs, it's a reflection of the camera's flash off the red blood cells of the vascular layer behind the retina.)

Night drives are also popular they provide the best chance of seeing the more rarely sighted nocturnal life of the bush: leopards, hyenas, rooikats, genets, civets, aardvarks, pangolins, bush pigs, African wild cats, cute hopping spring hares and the like. Plus, of course, all the game commonly seen during the day.

One shareholder was on a night drive with a nervous lady guest in charge of the spotlight. Suddenly the spot illuminated a solid mass of elephants standing in the road dead ahead. The elephants panicked and the spotlight holder even more. She switched off the spot. Now the shareholder behind the wheel hadn't a clue as to where the elephants were…charging, standing their ground, or retreating? As seeing the road immediately ahead is a necessity on rough and rocky roads, the Cruiser's headlights were angled downwards and did not reach very far at all.

The shareholder quickly tried to reverse so as to turn around on the narrow track but bumped into tree behind in the dark. He kept imploring the guest to put the spotlight back on, but she refused. Her reasoning was that "the elephants will see us!" Guess what lady, they absolutely could anyway… it's we humans who can't see in the dark!

The party arrived back at the lodge shaken (but thankfully not stirred by an angry elephant).

Chapter 20
FIRE! FIRE!

Being very hot and dry with vast areas of tall grassland and bushveld, much of Botswana is a tinderbox just waiting for a spark. The threat is such that Botswana law requires anyone asked to fight a fire must do so.

Our first major fire occurred soon after Estelle and I had moved into our newly finished Jwala home.

It had begun at a cattle-post just outside the top end of Jwala. A child reportedly tossed coals from the previous night's cooking fire into the bush. Wind had then fanned the coals to life and soon a major fire was moving down Jwala and into Zimbabwe's Tuli Circle. Mashatu and other Tuli Block reserves immediately sent staff to help us fight the kilometres-long fire front. There were no fire engines—just men armed with fire-beaters—long poles with a floppy, rubber, spade-shaped endpiece which, when wielded correctly, help stifle the flames by eliminating the oxygen that fire needs.

Radio calls to villages outside the Tuli Block resulted in two 5-ton trucks arriving, loaded with Botswanans who had answered the call for help. Almost before the trucks pulled up, the occupants, men and women, jumped out and ripped branches off the plentiful Mopani bushes to use them in place of fire-beaters. As soon as a branch became crisp from the flames, it was tossed away and another one harvested to carry on the fight. The temperature that day was well over 35 degrees Celcius, but in front of the flames, it must have been 45 degrees!

My job was to fill every available container with water at the lodge and drive my closed Land Cruiser to supply this essential liquid to the various firefighting teams. Several trips necessitated driving along narrow dirt tracks with flames licking the Cruiser on both sides. The appreciation of the thirsty firefighters made it so worthwhile.

Eventually, the fire was stopped just a kilometre from our house and the Jwala lodge, although it continued to burn in Zimbabwe.

A lasting memory of that day was the number of birds circling above our heads feasting on the insects that had taken to the air to avoid the flames. A huge insect braai that drongos, bee-eaters, rollers and their ilk took full advantage of.

Elephant dung is packed with undigested vegetation and can continue to harbour heat for hours. So, the late afternoon was spent walking through burnt areas kicking open and stamping on smouldering dung balls to ensure they wouldn't start a new fire. The ground was so hot it burnt the stitching and melted the glue in the treads of my bush boots, leaving me with soles that flapped with every step just like a Charlie Chaplin impersonator.

Unfortunately, there were some casualties that day…but none to the firefighters, thank goodness. Some tortoises and snakes failed to escape the flames. But the biggest loss was the massive, long-dead Leadwood tree that housed a large platform some 5 meters off the ground. From that platform, one could see for miles around. It also overlooked a small waterhole fed from a borehole.

Before its demise, Estelle and I had spent many fabulous hours on that platform watching herds of eland, kudu, impala, wildebeest, and zebra arrive to drink. Baboons, warthogs, ostriches and jackals were also frequent visitors. This popular waterhole also attracted lion due to a small rocky outcrop to one side of it that provided excellent cover behind which lions could hide until the right opportunity to rush at prey drinking at the pool presented itself.

Initially we left Caesar in the vehicle when we spent time on that platform, but when he once took himself off to drink at the waterhole, it became apparent that he needed to be up on the platform with us and out of harm's way! We bought a large hold-all bag, popped him into it and with the strap over my neck and shoulder I would carry him up the ladder. Of course, that was great when he was a puppy, but he was getting larger and heavier with each trip to Jwala. On one occasion when close to the top, the strap broke. I grabbed his girth with one arm, and amazingly he froze, allowing me to heave him onto the platform. If he had panicked or struggled, I doubt if I would have been able to hold onto him. What a clever boy. As the 4 x 3 metre platform had no railings or sides, Caesar kept away from the edges and just settled down, happy to be next to us.

One day, Estelle and I were sunbathing naked on that platform when a vehicle full of shareholders drove up out of the blue. With nowhere to hide, we wriggled into shirts and shorts while trying to keep flat on the wood planks to preserve some dignity!

On another occasion, we decided to get to the platform by dawn. No animals in sight. But a sort of croaking noise was coming from the direction of the waterhole. There was a damp swampy area far away to the southwest of Jwala where toads could be found in the rainy season, but I couldn't imagine that one had trekked across miles of baking bush and found this tiny waterhole. So I decided to climb down the ladder and walk down to the waterhole to see what might be making this strange sound. Halfway down the ladder, I heard Estelle calling me back with a whisper, "Lion!" she was saying as quietly as she could. I climbed back to the platform and saw a fine young lioness making her way from behind the rocky outcrop and padding her way to the water. Her paws and face were covered with the fresh red blood of a kill. She spotted my movement and stared intently at us for what seemed to be an unacceptably long time.

"Do you think she is seeing if there's a way to get up to us?" Estelle whispered. "Do you think she can get up here?" came next.

I did not think she could or would, but the atmosphere was extremely tense. Then, much to our surprise, a second equally bloody young lioness emerged from behind the rocks and made her way to the water. The first lioness relaxed and ignored us. A few minutes, later a young male lion sauntered from behind the outcrop. His mane was just showing promising growth. The three were undoubtedly littermates, still together after some 2 to 3 years. A later investigation behind the rocky outcrop showed that the three lions had killed a young eland early that morning and the grunting noise we had heard was that of the siblings growling at each other while feasting. Just as well I was not looking for a toad at the water's edge while they were enjoying breakfast.

Anyway…that giant dead Leadwood was the biggest casualty of the fire. Unbeknown to anyone, the fire had managed to penetrate the root system and a week later reached the great body of the old tree. Despite pouring water into every nook and cranny, we could not douse the main heat source, and after 3 more weeks the giant fell.

But the fire story did not end there. A month or two later, the Zimbabwean government dispatched a bulldozer plus two operators with supplies and a tent, to re-scrape the cutline between Botswana and Zimbabwe. The goal was obviously to clear a wider fire break to prevent another run-away veldfire from entering the Tuli Circle. However, on night two, the tent evidently caught alight, and new fire spread into Zimbabwe! Fortuitously, the wind direction pushed it away from Jwala this time! We did spend some evenings watching the progress of the flames inching across the bush towards the Zimbabwe horizon. We all wondered how the bulldozer team was going to explain this fire event.

Chapter 21
Just Love the Locals

Generally, Botswanans are salt-of-the-earth folk. Peaceful and respectful of everyone.

Botswana is an amazing country…not only a place of great African beauty with its vast deserts, flood plains like the famed Okavango Delta, vast grasslands dotted with rocky outcrops and, of course, its wildlife. But its people make it even more special. They must surely be some of the happiest and nicest folk on Earth.

Earlier on I introduced you to my much-valued building companion, Jim. His tiny village was situated on a gravel road on our way to Selibi Phikwe. Unlike so many South African rural villages liberally strewn with litter and strings of wind-blown, plastic bags caught on barbed wire fences, Jim's village was spotless. However, it transpired that this was largely due to the goat population that ate everything, including discarded cigarette packs, empty cement bags and any other rubbish including plastic bags!

Unfortunately, the track from the Tuli Block to Jim's village was not so pristine. So I decided to see if the village's little primary school might be interested in educational trips into the wildlife area. The warm and gushing headmistress was ecstatic. In rural Botswana, wildlife was viewed as problematic. Lions were only seen by villagers as killers of livestock, and the odd elephant that ventured into tribal land was a dreaded crop destroyer.

Determined to show the children and teachers the value of wildlife to Botswanans, I hatched a plan. On a monthly basis, I collected 10 excited kids and a teacher/supervisor/translator from the village school and travelled the bumpy road to the game reserve gate. First the children were divided into two teams and given score sheets. On the way to the game area, we would stop at litter patches and the team that collected the most litter was awarded points. Naturally, my captive audience was given a talk on the evil of littering at the same time! In the blazing Botswana sun, a sliver of broken glass can easily start a wildfire.

Once inside the reserve, the teams were given a bird book plus a list of the birds and wildlife we might see. The first team to identify a bird or animal got points with rare animals like lion, cheetah and leopard earning the highest points. When watching the spotting game, I would talk about each animal... such as wildebeest babies being able to gallop alongside their mothers within just 20 minutes of being born, and how giraffes give birth while standing up. And I drummed home the importance of wildlife areas to attract tourists to Botswana and thus create jobs for the surrounding villagers.

Part of the trip was a treat of an impala stew luncheon specially made by the Jwala staff. On one occasion I had quietly approached the hide overlooking the Jwala waterhole to call the headmistress and the children to the lapa for lunch when I heard the headmistress saying, "Can you eat this animal? And can you eat that one?" as impala, warthog and zebra arrived at the water.

So, thinking it might be good to see what the kids were actually learning from these trips, I handed out small leaflets for them to complete once back at school.

Bearing in mind that English is a second language to these primary school children, their responses were sometimes hilarious:

Q. What was the best thing you learnt today?

A. *That giraffes have a bath standing up.*

Q. Why are game reserves important to Botswana?

A. *Because wild animals attack tourists.* (Think that was meant to read "attract" tourists.)

When travelling to Selibi Phikwe to draw staff salaries or such, we always gave local hitchhikers a lift, all of whom offered a Pula or two as payment, which we never took. Caesar willingly accepted these new passengers and would snuggle up to them, much to their horror! One hitchhiker would not get into the backseat but insisted on sitting right at the back. Only once he was inside did we realise why. He had obviously not had the luxury of a bath for some months! We carried on with all the windows open to their maximum.

I once had occasion to spend time in a police station in Simolale waiting for a vehicle licence form to be completed. I sat on the wood bench in reception alongside a young man. We were both offered water. I declined but my companion accepted. A bit later, the youngster was offered food. This was also accepted. He was eventually escorted out of the room. The officer at the counter clicked his tongue. "That boy," he explained, "he killed his mother this morning…hacked her to death with a panga."

Would a violent murderer be treated with such empathy anywhere else in the world?

Chapter 22
Leaving Botswana for a New Life

Our prime reason for leaving was that we had been granted what was termed a 'Temporary' Permanent Resident's Permit by the Botswana government. It was valid for four years.

As our permit was due to expire, we sold our share in Jwala, our fully furnished house and our old game-viewing Land Cruiser and thereby raised the funds needed to set up a new chapter of our life back in South Africa. On a visit to the Cape some months earlier, in a tiny seaside village called Rooi Els in the Western Cape, we had found a most unusual, character-filled house perched on rocks above the waves. We bought it and were set to become the eleventh 'permanent' residents of Rooi Els. We needed a gradual reintroduction to society!

But days before we left Jwala for good, Caesar got badly beaten up. Not by a leopard, lion or a pack of hyenas. The managerial couple, from a nearby reserve in which we also had a share, asked us if we would look after their two Rottweilers while they took some time off in South Africa. Unfortunately, the Rotties were not good at sharing and a fight over impala legs ensued. Estelle rushed Caesar the 200 kilometres to the nearest vet. Our poor dog was bleeding from two deep, parallel gashes across his forehead. I watched the Cruiser drive off with Caesar looking like a gypsy with his head swathed in tea-towels to try and limit blood loss.

Returning the next day, Caesar resembled a canine version of Dr Frankenstein's monster. He had drainage tubes sticking out of his neck and head. The skin between the two gashes across the top of his head had been removed due to lack of blood supply and his whole forehead, from ear to ear, was shaved and crowned with a mass of stitches and more drainage tubes. He looked as though he had had an extreme facelift. But he'd survived!

Something we will never forget was our last evening at Jwala. The staff had invited us to join them around a fire in the secure, fenced staff village that we had built together. Estelle and I took all the clothes, linen and tinned foods, etc. that we no longer needed or could not fit into our trailer and laid them out for the staff to help themselves. Much excitement ensued. Finally, in the gentle glow of the lapa fire, we were given a heart-breaking serenade by all the staff. "Farewell, go well," they sang over and over again in soulful and beautiful harmony. We all shed a tear or twenty.

Early the next morning, just two days after Caesar's facelift, we left for Jwala for good and returned to South Africa. Everything we owned was packed into our trusty one-ton trailer and our closed Land Cruiser. And with minds packed equally full of wonderful memories, we drove away…

It was not an easy trip. The distance to Rooi Els was 2,000 kilometres! We had Caesar's dog basket wedged on the front passenger seat and Estelle sat behind with Lucky, the white cat that we had brought to Jwala from Johannesburg. Lucky seemed determined to voice his displeasure all the way. In desperation, Estelle eventually let him out of his carrier and all he wanted was to sit up front in Caesar's basket. Caesar retreated to the backseat.

Once in South Africa and therefore within cell-phone signal, we called a friend to say we were on our way…but while speaking, FLAP, FLAP, FLAP and swerve—a trailer tyre had punctured and we had to pull over. Needless to say. all the tools necessary to change the wheel were neatly packed away in the back compartment of the Cruiser under half our belongings! Thankfully, after unloading everything, changing the wheel and repacking, the trip continued uneventfully.

That evening outside Bloemfontein, and still some 1,000 kilometres from our destination, we looked for a motel that would allow a dog. (I thought it best not to mention a cat!) We succeeded. The second day of the great trek was less eventful and lucky for us, Lucky was less noisy.

By dusk, we drove into the driveway our new house in Rooi Els. We did wonder what the few neighbours must have thought of the mud-coated overloaded Land Cruiser, towing a heavily laden 1-ton trailer with a 3.2-meter carved wooden giraffe roped to the top and a mountain bike tied to each side. Plus, there was the curiosity of Dr Frankenstein's dog!

But the next morning, a lovely lady walked down from a house overlooking ours, carrying a welcoming bottle of wine…so we had obviously not made too bad an impression. In fact, Rooi Els proved to be a stunning place to live.

The Kein Hangklip mountain reared up right behind our new home and the waves crashed just in front. The Atlantic Ocean became an escape into a new and wonderful wilderness for me filled with striped pyjama sharks, octopus, weird fishes and plentiful crayfish that lurked amongst the kelp roots on the rocky ocean floor!

In crayfish season (and armed with a permit), I took to donning a double-thick wetsuit and braved the crashing waves with crayfish nets baited with fish-heads. Often hyperthermia would begin to set in by the time four legal-size crayfish were in my pouch. Although squeamish about killing the crayfish (one puts them in fresh water and they just go to sleep, permanently), they were just so yummy when halved, slathered with garlic butter and popped on the braai!

Life in Rooi Els was good. Much, much quieter than Johannesburg and with telephones, electricity, shops, doctors and friends less than 30 minutes away, far, far easier than our years in the bush…

But we are forever thankful for all our Botswana experiences, and now sharing them with you!